THE HIDDEN PATH OF THE TRIBES OF BRITAIN

Divination, Totems, and the Sacred
Wisdom of the Ancients

RICHARD SIMONIAN

First published 2025

TABLE OF CONTENTS

PROLOGUE

THE WHISPER BENEATH
THE SOIL

It all began, as many sacred things do, with a whisper. Not a loud, triumphant call, but something softer—something that stirred beneath the surface, like a seed cracking open underground. I didn't know then what it was, only that it came from somewhere ancient, earthy, and close to the bone. It was as if the land itself had begun to speak, not in words but in a language made of wind, moss, and memory.

My earliest guide on this path was my grandmother, a wise and quietly powerful woman from the West Country. She was not one to declare herself a teacher, but she was one nonetheless. Through her stories—told by the hearth, in the garden, or while walking the worn footpaths of her village— she passed on ways of seeing the world that didn't come from books or churches. She taught me that the land remembers, that stones hold stories, and that listening is an act of devotion. Her hands, always in the soil, seemed to carry the spirit of the land itself. I realise now she was sowing something in me from a young age, something I wouldn't come to fully understand until much later.

As I grew, I felt the pull of the old ways growing stronger. Not as nostalgia, but as a living presence—something urgent and alive. That yearning took me beyond the hedgerows and hills of Britain, across oceans and mountains, to teachers and elders who lived close to the earth and spirit. I sat with Q'ero shamans who sang to the Apus, the mountain spirits, and taught me to listen to the earth through breath and silence. Their medicine, rooted in reverence and reciprocity, awakened something familiar in me. From the frozen steppes of Siberia, I met shamans who knew the language of fire and drum. They spoke of soul retrieval, of crossing worlds, of healing not just the individual, but the lineage and the land. And from the heart of Africa, a wise man from the Kongo shared with me the teachings of Catechesis—not in the way it's known through colonised lenses, but as an embodied, ancestral transmission rooted in community, spirit, and song.

These traditions didn't replace what I had learned from my grandmother—they illuminated it. They affirmed what I had always known deep down: that beneath the overlay of modern life, beneath even the ruins of Rome and the legacy of Saxon steel, lies something older. A living path. A thread of wisdom carried by the land and by the bones of those who walked it before us.

This book was not born out of curiosity alone, but out of a calling. A calling to help people return. Not to retreat into the past, but to remember a way of being that predates conquest and dogma. A way rooted in relationship—to land, to spirit, to story. Before churches were built upon the springs. Before sacred groves were felled in the name of empires. Before our ancestors' tongues were reshaped by foreign kings. There was a knowing, and that knowing was enough.

We have been taught to forget. Taught to see land as property, spirit as superstition, and history as something that begins with Rome. But the land has not forgotten. Nor have the old spirits. They wait, as they always have, in the folds of the hills, the curves of the rivers, the silence of the woods. They are not angry—only patient. They speak still, to those who know how to listen.

The voice of the land is not always easy to hear. It doesn't shout. It doesn't demand. But if you spend enough time beneath the trees, beside the streams, or sitting in silence on an ancient hill, it begins to come through. At first, it may feel like a memory you never lived, a dream that stays with you long after waking. But in time, it becomes clearer. The land speaks through your bones. Through that ache in your chest when you see a hawk wheel above a barrow. Through the sudden stillness that falls over you when you step into a grove where no sound seems to enter. The voice of the land is layered—part spirit, part ancestor, part something that simply is. It doesn't need translation, only presence.

And it is through that presence that the memory of the old tribes stirs. Not as distant figures from a history book, but as kin. As guardians. As echoes in your blood. They didn't leave us; we left them. And yet, they have waited. Their memory is not preserved in museums, but in the lines of the hills, the shape of standing stones, and in the language of totems: the hare, the hawk, the adder, the toad. Each one a symbol, a doorway, a guide.

The old tribes didn't see themselves as separate from the land. They didn't walk on it—they walked with it. Every hill had a story. Every river had a name that was more than a label; it was a spell, a song, a spirit. Their ceremonies were not performed to impose order on nature, but to remain in right relationship with it. Their wisdom was rooted in observation, in reciprocity, in knowing the seasons of the soul as surely as the seasons of the soil.

To remember them is not simply an act of reverence. It is an act of healing. For they knew what we are only now beginning to remember: that we are not lost, only disconnected. That the silence we feel inside is not emptiness, but the space where something ancient is waiting to rise.

So let this be your invitation.

If you have ever stood barefoot in the grass and felt a presence rise from the earth to meet you, If you have ever wept for a world you cannot name but still remember, If you have ever dreamt of wolves or heard your name in the wind, Then this book is for you.

It is for the wanderers who never quite felt at home in modern life. It is for those who feel something stir when they see a full moon rising or hear a raven cry. It is for the ones who feel drawn to ruins, to stones, to trees that have seen centuries. It is for those who sense that our ancestors left something for us to find, hidden in plain sight.

This is not a how-to guide. It is a map of remembering.

Each chapter is a step. Each story, a stone on the path. Each ritual, a doorway.

And you do not walk it alone.

The land walks with you. The old ones walk with you. And perhaps, most importantly, your truest self walks with you—the one who has always known the way.

So welcome. To the whisper beneath the soil. To the path beneath the path. To the place where the tribes still speak. To the hidden way that is not lost—only waiting to be found.

PART I

CHAPTER 01

ALBION BEFORE THE CROWN

Before Britain was named, before the Saxon kings, the stone churches, or the Roman roads, there was a land known by another name—Albion. It is a name that echoes through poetry and myth, more spirit than label, more dream than geography. Albion was not a country but a condition, a living landscape shaped by rivers, forests, barrows, and sacred stones. And at the heart of this older world were the people we have come to call the Beaker folk.

The Beaker people are among the most mysterious and influential cultures to have shaped prehistoric Britain. Their name, given by modern archaeologists, comes from the distinctive pottery vessels found in their burial sites—"beakers," with wide mouths and intricate geometric designs. But the word "beka," as some oral traditions suggest, may have deeper roots—a reference to the double-edged axe or pickaxe many of these people carried. One side for breaking earth, the other honed for protection or combat. A tool of builders, yes, but also of warriors and earth-keepers. It was more than just a practical object; it was a symbol of duality: creation and destruction, cultivation and defence, sacred work and sacred war.

The Beaker culture emerged during the late Neolithic period and spread across much of western Europe before firmly taking root in the British Isles around 2500 BCE. They were not the first inhabitants of Britain, but their arrival marked a turning point. Their settlements, craftsmanship, and social practices began to reshape the culture of these lands in ways that would echo through millennia. They brought with them metallurgy, new forms of burial, and most importantly, a cosmology that understood the land as a living entity—a place woven with spirit and meaning.

The sacred relationship the Beaker people had with the land was not symbolic—it was lived. They sensed, intuitively, that the landscape had memory, that the earth breathed. Their monuments and settlements reflect this understanding. Many of the most iconic megalithic sites in Britain—Stonehenge, Avebury, Castlerigg, and countless others—were either originally constructed or significantly altered during the Beaker era. These were not isolated structures, but part of a greater spiritual landscape. The placement of stones, the alignment with solar and lunar cycles, the use of natural geological features—all were intentional. These sacred places were built at energetic nodes, places where ley lines crossed, where the veil between worlds was thinnest.

These circles were not simply for observing the heavens. They were for dialogue with the otherworld. Rituals were held to honour ancestors, seek guidance, or align with the shifting balance of seasons. The Beaker folk read the sky like a text, not to dominate it, but to move with it. The solstices and equinoxes were not merely calendar events—they were spiritual gateways. These people tracked the moon's cycle with careful attention, their ceremonies often echoing its waxing and waning. The hare, often seen in the full moon's light, likely held great spiritual significance. The land's creatures were never just animals; they were messengers and kin.

Their homes reflected this sacred geometry. Roundhouses built of timber and thatch followed the same circular pattern found in their stone works. There was no corner to hide in, no edge to separate. These spaces, warmed by central hearths, reinforced the idea that life was a cycle—a return to source. The fire in the middle was not just for warmth. It was the heart, the soul, the sun brought down into the dwelling. Families gathered in these circular sanctuaries to share stories, honour the dead, and pass on wisdom. Songs and chants carried through smoke and flickering shadows, echoing the rhythm of the earth itself.

Much has been written about their burial practices—and rightly so. The Beaker folk shifted from communal burial mounds to individual graves. These graves often contained personal items: beakers, tools, blades, ornaments. The body, carefully positioned in a foetal pose, was laid on its side facing the rising sun. This orientation suggests a rebirth, a return, a passage. Death was not an end, but a reentry into the womb of the earth. Women, men, elders, and children were all buried with reverence. Some graves are marked with great precision, indicating individuals of importance—perhaps spiritual leaders or seers.

Archaeological evidence shows that some women were buried with prestige items—bracelets, amber beads, and even metalworking tools. This hints at a culture where wisdom and power were not solely the domain of men. Perhaps they had clan mothers or moon priestesses, women who guarded the mysteries and sang the stories of the tribe. The spiritual authority of women in pre-Roman Britain has often been overlooked, but traces remain—in myth, in burial, and in folk memory.

The Beaker people were metalworkers of surprising sophistication. They brought copper and gold into ritual use, eventually giving rise to the Bronze Age. They knew how to transform what was hidden in the earth into tools, weapons, and symbols of power. This act—turning ore into blade or ornament—was not merely technological; it was magical. It required knowledge, patience, and spiritual guidance. To strike the right balance of elements, to shape metal with flame and stone, was to echo the great cosmic alchemy of sun and soil.

Beyond metallurgy, their understanding of the natural world was profound. They moved with the herds, respected the cycles of plants, and cultivated relationships with animals not as masters, but as fellow beings. Cattle and sheep were not just food sources—they were part of the living economy of the land. Seasonal migrations, harvest festivals, and rites of passage marked their calendar. These were not separate events, but woven into the rhythm of life.

The Beaker people were engineers of memory. Their settlements and monuments formed a living map. Their seasonal feasts marked the cycles of the year—Samhain, Imbolc, Beltane, and Lughnasadh likely had predecessors in Beaker society, echoing older rhythms long before they were named. At these gatherings, they told stories, shared food, and honoured the ancestors and spirits who made the land fertile and the community strong. Music and dance were woven into ceremony—drumming that mimicked the heartbeat of the earth, chanting that drew breath from the wind.

They were also dreamers. Many of their burial mounds and sacred places are connected to legends of sleeping heroes or gods beneath the hills. These tales, passed down through generations, whisper of a time when the living and the dead walked closer, when the stars had names, and animals spoke in symbols. The Beaker people did not need to write their stories—they lived them. Every path, every stone, every mound was a verse.

Their influence did not vanish. It passed, subtly but surely, into the tribal cultures that followed: the Dumnonii, the Dobunni, the Durotriges, and others. These tribes inherited the sacred places, the knowledge of the stars, the reverence for the circle and the hearth. The later Druids would walk the paths the Beaker people cleared. Folk customs, rituals around wells and stones, offerings left at trees—these are echoes. Threads in a long weaving.

We often think history begins with written words. But there is another history, written in placement and pattern, in bones and broken pots, in paths through the forest and hollows in the hills. The Beaker folk did not build empires, but they built belonging. They did not write laws, but they shaped memory. They are not remembered in chronicles, but in the way a stone casts its shadow at dawn.

Their roads, wrongfully credited to Rome, were ancient even in Caesar's time. These trackways connected hillforts, river crossings, sacred wells. They were not built with concrete, but with intention. To walk such a path today is to feel something stir. You are not alone. You are walking the old lines.

What remains is not ruin but reminder. The Beaker people remind us that civilisation need not mean domination. That sacredness lives in how we build, where we walk, and what we remember. They remind us that the land is not empty, and the past is not silent.

They did not vanish. They changed. Their memory lives in the Durotriges, the Dobunni, the Brigantes, the countless tribes that emerged and held their own sacred ways. Their bones became the hills. Their paths became the ley lines. Their songs became the wind.

Albion remembers.

This is the beginning. The threshold. The doorway back to the old path. Before the crown. Before the kings. Before forgetting.

This is Albion. And it still remembers.

History of Brutus and the Land of Albion

Introduction

In the tapestry of Britain's origin myths, few figures loom as large as Brutus of Troy and the primeval realm of Albion. The tale of Brutus – a fugitive Trojan prince who voyaged across unknown seas to found a new kingdom – was cherished for centuries as the very root of British history. Medieval chroniclers and bards wove this mytho-historical narrative to connect Britain with the glories of antiquity. By linking the Britons to the heroes of Troy and the lineage of Aeneas, the story of Brutus bestowed upon the island an epic ancestry and a sense of destiny. It became more than legend: it was ancestral memory and spiritual metaphor, used to define British identity and kingship in profound ways. Over time, this legend of Brutus conquering Albion – the old name for Britain – evolved into a rich tapestry integrating Trojan and Roman heritage, Celtic and druidic lore, and the mysterious presence of pre-Celtic giants. It inspired medieval monarchs, Tudor propagandists, and Renaissance poets alike. In this chapter, we will expand the history of Brutus and the land of Albion, exploring how this origin myth connects to broader traditions and how it influenced Britain's view of itself as a sacred land and kingdom. We will journey from ancient Troy to the white cliffs of Albion, tracing the legend's development through chronicles and its later echoes in esoteric lore and poetry. The narrative will blend historical commentary with spiritual reflection, showing how the myth of Brutus became a vessel for Britain's collective imagination.

Trojan Origins: Brutus's Ancestry and Epic Journey

Brutus's story begins in the ashes of the Trojan War, linking Britain's founders to one of the most famed sagas of the ancient world. According to medieval legend, Brutus (or *Brut*) was a great-grandson of Aeneas of Troy, making him part of the same royal line that, in Roman mythology, founded Rome itself

This elegant connection meant that the Britons could claim kinship with the Romans and the heroes of Homer. The legend first surfaced in early medieval texts like the *Historia Brittonum* (c. 9th century) and was later elaborated by Geoffrey of Monmouth in his 12th-century *History of the Kings of Britain.*

In these accounts, Brutus's saga unfolds like a miniature epic. He is born in Italy generations after the fall of Troy, a time when Aeneas's descendants are establishing themselves. As fate would have it, Brutus fulfils a dark prophecy at a young age: while hunting, he accidentally kills his father, an act of misfortune that leads to his banishment. Exiled from his kin, Brutus wanders in search of a new home. He first journeys through the Mediterranean, retracing in reverse the path of his ancestor Aeneas. In one version, he sails among the islands of the Tyrrhenian Sea and eventually lands in a part of Greece where he discovers a community of Trojan refugees enslaved by the Greeks. Brutus, though still young, proves himself a natural leader: his courage, skill, and noble lineage win the Trojans' trust they plead with him to become their leader and deliverer from thraldom.

Embracing this call, Brutus raises a rebellion against the local Greek king, Pandrasus. Through a series of guerrilla battles and a daring nighttime raid on the Greek camp, Brutus's band triumphs against the odds and King Pandrasus is captured, and Brutus negotiates freedom for all the Trojan captives. The defeated king even offers his daughter, *Ignoge (Innogen)*, in marriage to Brutus as part of the peace terms, along with ships and supplies for the Trojans to depart safely

With his new bride and his liberated people, Brutus sets sail to find the land that will become their promised home. The image of Brutus and Innogen embarking together, as shown in a 15th-century tapestry, beautifully captures this hopeful moment.

According to Geoffrey of Monmouth's narrative, the Trojans roam across the Mediterranean in search of a prophesied isle. They briefly land on deserted islands; on one such island they discover a mysterious abandoned temple of Diana. Sensing divine guidance, Brutus performs sacred rites to the goddess of the hunt (and the moon), seeking a vision. That night, Diana appears to Brutus in a dream, delivering a prophecy that has echoed in British lore

In that medieval depiction, Brutus (center, crowned) stands at the prow of the ship with Innogen beside him, as musicians trumpeting in red caps signal departure. It is a visual echo of Virgil's *Aeneid*, now with a distinctly British destiny on the horizon.

ever since. She tells him of a green western island, long uninhabited by men, where his destiny awaits:

"Brutus! There lies beyond the stormy seas
A realm amid the Ocean, walled by waves;
An island, lush and fair, where giants dwelled.
Seek that westward Isle of Albion; there
Thy descendants shall rise, and kings be born,
To rule a nation blessed and free."

Thus encouraged, Brutus and his people set sail westward with renewed purpose. The voyage is not without further adventures. Geoffrey's history notes that they passed by the Pillars of Hercules into the Atlantic and even had a perilous encounter with sirens on the sea

They also stop in Gaul (France), where Brutus's companion, the mighty warrior Corineus, provokes a conflict with Goffar, king of Aquitaine, after hunting in his forests. A fierce war in Gaul ensues; though the Trojans fight valiantly and even found the city of Tours in memory of Brutus's fallen nephew Turonus, they are vastly outnumbered. Deciding not to press their luck further in Gaul, Brutus leads his people back to the ships and sails onward.

At last, the Trojans reach the shores of Albion – the mysterious island foretold by the goddess. They land at the place known today as Totnes, in Devon, according to later tradition in Totnes, a small granite boulder called the "Brutus Stone" still marks the legendary spot where Brutus first stepped ashore, proclaiming: *"Here I stand, and here I rest. And this land shall be called Britain"*

Indeed, upon setting foot on the island, Brutus ceremonially renamed Albion to "Britain", after himself, and declared his followers the Britons, giving his name to the people and the land. This act of naming is portrayed as a moment of destiny: a Trojan prince christening a new nation that would carry forward the legacy of fallen Troy. In Geoffrey's account, Brutus soon established a capital city on the banks of the Thames – calling it Troia Nova ("New Troy") – which would later be known as Trinovantum and eventually London.

There, Brutus is said to have built a palace and, significantly, a temple to the goddess Diana on what is now Ludgate Hill. Medieval legend holds that the very site of St.

Paul's Cathedral was once Brutus's temple of Diana, and that the London Stone was an altar from that shrine, such lore illustrates how deeply the Brutus myth became entwined with the sacred geography of London's later landscape.

Having founded his city and kingdom, Brutus ruled as the first king of the Britons for 24 years, according to the chronicles. When he died, the island was divided among his three sons, each ruling a part of Britain named after them: Locrinus took Loegria (England), Albanactus took Alba (Scotland), and Kamber took Kambria (Wales). In this way, the entire island and its future peoples were bound together by common parentage in Brutus – a powerful symbol that all Britons (whether Welsh, Scots, or English) were one family in origin. This division also neatly explained the ancient names of regions (for example, "Albion" and "Albany" from Albanactus). Brutus himself was laid to rest in his beloved New Troy (London), and so the legendary era of Britain's founding began.

It is important to note that medieval chroniclers synchronised Brutus's story with biblical and historical timelines to give it credibility. The *Historia Brittonum* asserts that Brutus arrived in Britain when Eli was the High Priest of Israel and the Ark of the Covenant was captured by the Philistines roughly around the time of the Judges in the Old Testament. This would place Brutus's migration many centuries before the Romans, anchoring British history in an epoch as hoary as the times of Samuel. Such synchronisation with scripture was intentional: it wove the pagan myth into a Christian framework. By aligning Brutus with the era of Biblical heroes, medieval writers implied that Britain's story ran parallel to those of the oldest known civilisations, emphasising that the Britons were an ancient people with a destiny, not mere latecomers on the stage of history.

Thus, by the High Middle Ages, the narrative of Brutus of Troy had become the accepted starting point of British history in numerous accounts. It provided an epic foundation myth: a wandering prince, guided by the gods, finding a promised land and establishing a nation. This myth gave medieval Britons a sense of profound antiquity and heroic origin. They were not simply descendants of barbarian tribes; they were, in their own national story, descendants of Trojans, cousins to the Romans, and heirs of a divine mandate delivered by Diana. The legend's broad appeal lay in this fusion of classical heroism and providential design, which cast Albion as a new Troy and its people as a chosen line destined for greatness.

Albion Before Brutus: Giants and the Lost Realm

When Brutus and his Trojans first landed on Albion's shores, they found a land of wild, primeval beauty – and a land inhabited not by civilised men, but by giants. Medieval legend holds that giants were the only inhabitants of Albion at that time. Geoffrey of Monmouth recounts that upon the Trojans' arrival, they encountered "a few giants" roaming the forests and hills, descendants of an earlier age. Brutus's comrade Corineus took great delight in battling these fearsome natives. In the most famous episode, the largest giant – Gogmagog – was kept alive so that Corineus could wrestle him in single combat. The duel took place during a celebratory feast, and in the end the warrior hurled the giant from a cliff, dashing him on the rocks below. Local lore places this showdown at Plymouth Hoe in Devon, a site still associated with the giant's fall. With Gogmagog's demise, the last of Albion's giants were subdued, leaving the island fully in Brutus's control.

Yet Geoffrey never explained where these giants came from, nor how Albion got its name in the first place. This gap in the story perplexed later medieval writers. To fill the void, an origin myth of Albion's giants emerged in the 14th century – a legend as fantastical as it is revealing. According to a popular tale recorded in the Anglo-Norman poem *Des Grantz Geanz* ("Of the Great Giants") and later English chronicles, the story goes that Albion was named after a woman: the exiled princess Albina. In this myth, Albina was the eldest of 30 or 33 sisters, daughters of a Syrian (or Greek) king often mis-identified as "Diocletian". These princesses were said to be proud, independent, and unwilling to be forced into arranged marriages. When their father married them off against their will, the rebellious sisters conspired to murder their husbands on their wedding night rather than submit to them. Albina led this grim plot. The plan was largely successful – they slew their husbands – but their father discovered the crime. As punishment, he ordered the murderous daughters to be set adrift at sea in a ship without sails or oars, leaving their fate to the waves. After a long and desperate voyage, the boat miraculously washed ashore on a distant uninhabited island – the island of Albion. There, the sisters became the first human inhabitants.

Isolated on this wild isle with no men around, Albina and her sisters supposedly consorted with demons (incubi) or evil spirits, and as a result they birthed a race of giants. These giants – enormous, brutish, and lawless – multiplied and roamed Albion for generations. The island took its name from Princess Albina, commemorating the leader of these wayward women who had populated it. Fast forward to Brutus's arrival: the giants he and his Trojans encountered were none other than the descendants of Albina's accursed lineage. In some versions of the tale, when Brutus captures Gogmagog, he actually interrogates the giant about his origins. The giant Gogmagog then recounts this entire story – tracing his people back to Albina – thereby explaining to Brutus (and the reader) how Albion came to be inhabited by giants and named after a woman

This Albina legend is a fascinating complement to the Brutus myth. It serves several purposes in medieval storytelling. First, it explained the etymology of *Albion* (a name of obscure origin) by connecting it to a person, Albina. Second, it provided a sort of *"pre-history"* of Britain – a time before Brutus – satisfying the impulse to imagine an even deeper antiquity for the island. And third, it introduced a moral allegory: Albina and her sisters represent chaos, disobedience, and primordial sin (murdering husbands and mating with demons), whereas Brutus represents order, civilisation, and divine sanction arriving to tame the land. Thus, when Brutus and his Trojans vanquish the giants, it symbolises the triumph of a new divinely ordained age over an older, darker era.

Regardless of its exact origins, the tale became popular. By the 15th century, many British chronicles began with Albina and the giants, then segued into Brutus – effectively layering one myth upon another. In these retellings, Albion was a land prepared (in a rough way) for Brutus's coming: the giants cleared away any previous human society, and their eventual defeat by Brutus's people allowed a fresh start.

Beyond the Albina myth, there were even more archaic whispers about Albion. The Greek myths of Heracles

(Hercules) mention a giant named Albion, said to be a son of the sea-god Poseidon. According to Greek storytellers, Hercules, during his own wanderings, encountered two giant brothers named Albion and Bergion in a far-off western land and slew them with the help of Zeus

Renaissance chroniclers like Raphael Holinshed were aware of these classical references and sometimes folded them into the narrative. Holinshed writes that Neptune's son Albion was given rule over the island of Britain (thus explaining the name), until Hercules came and killed Albion and his brother for their tyranny. He also mentions another ancient people called "Samotheans" who supposedly dwelt in Albion even before the giants, led by a son of Japheth named Samothes. These intricate variations show the lengths to which writers went to antique the history of Britain – pushing its origin further back by adding successive layers of legend. In effect, Britain's legendary history became a palimpsest: first Samothes (a purely invented figure), then Albion the giant, then Albina and her giant offspring, and finally Brutus and the Trojans, each one conquering or succeeding the former.

For our purposes, the key takeaway is how pre-Celtic "lineages" were imagined in myth. Historically, we know Britain had pre-Celtic inhabitants (Neolithic peoples, builders of Stonehenge, etc.), and Celtic Britons arrived later. The medieval mind translated this dim awareness of "others before us" into folklore of giants and foreign princesses. Giants, in many cultures, often symbolise the primordial forces or earlier races of the land. In Britain, they became a convenient stand-in for those mysterious predecessors: ancient, formidable, but ultimately swept aside by the divinely favoured newcomers (in this case, Brutus's Trojans). Even the megalithic monuments, whose origins were unknown, were ascribed to giants or to Merlin's magic in these legends. Geoffrey of Monmouth himself claimed Stonehenge was built by giants (transported from Africa to Ireland, then to Salisbury by Merlin's sorcery), which aligns with the notion that only giants could have lifted the huge stones. So the "giants of Albion" in the Brutus tale can be seen as a mythologized memory of Britain's pre-Celtic past – a past that had to be overthrown to make way for civilisation.

In summary, by the time Brutus renames Albion as Britain, the mythic narrative suggests he is cleansing and redefining the land. He inherits an island marred by the violence of Albina's progeny, and by defeating the giants and giving the land his name, he sanctifies it for a new people. This sets the stage for all subsequent British history (legendary and real) to unfold on a land that was now theirs by conquest and divine destiny. The story of Albion's prior giants contributes a rich layer of depth to the Brutus mythos – painting Britain as not just an empty stage, but a once-untamed realm that had awaited its rightful guardians. It also reinforced an idea that would recur in later thought: that Britain (Albion) was a special land, set apart since the dawn of time, its very soil imbued with myth and meaning even before its formal "founding."

Brutus and the Tapestry of Ancestry: Trojan, Roman, and Divine Lineages

One reason the legend of Brutus gained such currency was that it plugged the British into the grand "family tree" of the known world. In medieval scholarly tradition, it was important to trace peoples back to the sons of Noah from the Bible (Shem, Ham, and Japheth) as well as to famous classical heroes. The Britons, through Brutus, managed to do both.

Trojan Lineage: First and foremost, Brutus is touted as a descendant of Aeneas, the Trojan prince who survived Troy's fall. Different sources made Brutus either a grandson or great-grandson of Aeneas. For example, Geoffrey explicitly calls Brutus the son of Silvius, who was the son of Ascanius (the son of Aeneas). In any case, the precise genealogy was less important than the connection it gave: Aeneas -> Ascanius -> Brutus. By this link, the Britons become cousins to the Romans, since Aeneas's son Ascanius (also called Iulus) was the legendary ancestor of the founders of Rome. As one medieval writer put it, Brutus "linked Britain to the history of Rome and its Empire"

This Trojan lineage bestowed immense prestige. In a time when ancient lineage equaled legitimacy, to say Britain's kings ultimately came from Troy was to put them in the same league as the Caesars (who traced their lineage to Aeneas via Romulus). It was a translatio imperii – the transfer of empire – from Troy westward to Rome and to Britain. The Matter of Britain became a sibling to the Matter of Rome in medieval literature.

The Roman connection went beyond mere kinship. Medieval Britons knew that the Romans had conquered Britain under Caesar and Claudius. How to reconcile that historical fact with the legend that Trojan Britons were as noble as Romans? Some chroniclers finessed this by suggesting the Romans were reclaiming kindred territory since the Britons were of Trojan stock like themselves. Others emphasised that London (Troia Nova) was founded even before Rome's domination, implying Britain had an independent greatness. In *The Faerie Queene*, Edmund Spenser reflects this pride by having a character recount that Britain was settled by Trojans led by Brutus who built "Troy-novant" (New Troy) long before Caesar's arrival, meaning

London's mythical foundation preceded Roman London. The legend gave the English a way to boast that their capital's spiritual origins were as ancient as Rome's – if not more so – since it was a "New Troy" established by Trojans directly, free of Roman mediation.

Divine and Heroic Ancestry: Tied into the Trojan lineage is an implicit claim to divine ancestry. In Greco-Roman myth, Aeneas was the son of Venus (Aphrodite) and the mortal Anchises. That makes Brutus, as Aeneas's progeny, a descendant of a goddess – literally of divine blood. Medieval chronicles, written by Christian monks, usually downplayed overt pagan divinity. They did not often trumpet that "Britons have Venus's blood" (that would sound heretical). However, the notion of an exalted, quasi-divine origin still seeped through. The chronicles instead attempted to reconcile Trojan genealogy with the Bible. For instance, some versions in *Historia Brittonum* trace Brutus's lineage back to Japheth, son of Noah. One variant even says Brutus was descended from Ham (Noah's other son). These are efforts to fit Brutus into the Biblical framework: after the Flood, Japheth's line supposedly populated Europe, so Brutus must ultimately come from Japheth. Another curious variant made Brutus the great-grandson of Numa Pompilius, the second King of Rome, to graft him onto known Roman history. These conflicting genealogies (classical vs Biblical) show scholars struggling to place Brutus in both the sacred biblical history and secular heroic history. They recognised that the purely classical version (with pagan gods) conflicted with the Biblical timeline, so they offered "Christianised" pedigrees.

Regardless of the version, Brutus's ancestors were illustrious. By blood he was linked to kings and heroes of the ancient world – Priam's royal house of Troy, and through Aeneas to Dardanus (whom legends made a son of

Zeus/Jupiter). If one followed the Biblical line, through Japheth, the Britons could claim to descend from the line of Noah's sons that also gave rise to the Greeks and Romans. In fact, a common medieval construct was the idea that Japheth's grandsons included figures like Alanus, who had sons named Francus, Romanus, Britto (or Brutus), etc., each becoming the eponymous founder of a European people. One version in *Historia Brittonum* literally lists a Brutus son of Hisicion son of Alanus, brother to Francus (ancestor of the Franks), Alamanus (Germans), and Romanus (Romans). This "Frankish Table of Nations" was a fanciful way to give all major nations a common origin after the Flood. While confusing, it shows the intent: to include the Britons among the ordained nations of the world, not as an afterthought but as equals to the others in antiquity.

The upshot of all these ancestral claims was a powerful narrative: Brutus fit the archetype of the divinely-sanctioned founder. Much like Moses leading the Israelites to their promised land, or Aeneas journeying to found Rome by fate of the gods, Brutus was portrayed as a chosen instrument. The prophecy from Diana cemented this – it was as if the goddess (in Christian hindsight, perhaps God through a pagan oracle) had reserved Britain for Brutus's people. This gave the Britons a sense of manifest destiny. Later writers even drew explicit parallels between Britain and Israel. One 17th-century commentator mused that as Aeneas was to Rome, so Brutus was to Britain – and just as the Israelites had Joshua leading them to a promised land, Britain had Brutus. Some went further to claim Britons as a chosen people: an idea that gained weird new life in the 19th-century pseudo-historical movement of British Israelism. For instance, proponents like Wilson and Blackett (modern authors) argued that the Trojan migration led by Brutus might itself have been part of the dispersal of Israel's lost tribes – claiming (without historical basis) that the Trojan War and its exiles were tied to Israelite refugees. In their theory, Troy's fall (dated much later than historians accept) and Brutus's exodus were steps in God's plan to bring Israelites (in Trojan disguise) to Britain. This extreme interpretation never achieved mainstream credibility, but it illustrates how elastic and alluring the Brutus myth was for anyone wanting to cast Britain's origins as divinely guided. Whether through classical gods or Biblical God, Brutus's coming to Albion could be framed as an act of providence.

What did this mean for British identity? It meant that from the medieval viewpoint, the Britons (and later the English who adopted the myth) were not just a random tribe among many, but the product of a legendary ancestry as venerable as any on earth. This gave kings and chroniclers a rich source of political mythology. For the Welsh and Britons of the Middle Ages, it validated their claims against the upstart Saxons; for the English of the later Middle Ages and Renaissance, it gave them a backstory to rival that of any Continental nation.

One can imagine a bard or storyteller around a hearth or at a royal court proudly reciting: *"Our forefather was Brutus, kin of Aeneas, kin of gods; he sailed the seas like Ulysses, defeated giants, and planted Trojan seed in this soil. Thus are we the Britons, children of Troy and of destiny."* Such rhetoric bolstered sacred kingship too, because if kings could claim descent from Brutus, they effectively claimed the mantle of Troy and the blessings of Diana's prophecy. Many medieval kings of Brittonic lineage (e.g. Welsh princes) did indeed list Brutus at the top of their genealogies. This legendary pedigree was also carefully maintained in the genealogical rolls presented to English kings. For example, a roll for King Edward IV in the 15th century begins with Adam, then Noah's sons, down through Aeneas to Brutus and through the line of British kings up to Edward – mingling Biblical, Trojan, and British lines in one grand narrative.

In literature, the ancestry through Brutus allowed later heroes to shine even more. King Arthur, the greatest British hero, was said to descend in direct line from Brutus over many generations. That means Arthur's nobility and right to rule were literally anchored in this ancient Trojan blood. This is noted in chronicles and even in Spenser's *Faerie Queene*, where an allegorical genealogy in Book II traces the British monarchs from Brutus onward, stressing that Arthur (and by extension the Tudors) were "anciently derived from royal stock" of Troy. Likewise, London's mythical name "New Troy" gave poets a chance to praise the city as heir to the greatness of Ilium. All these ancestral threads – Trojan heroism, Roman kinship, divine favor – were woven into the national mythology through the figure of Brutus.

In sum, Brutus's lineage served as a bridge between worlds: the world of classical epics and the world of biblical patriarchs, the realm of pagan gods and the providence of the Christian God. It satisfied the ego of a nation to think that their first king was both a grandson of Venus and yet foreseen by Scripture (via aligning with times of the Judges). Such is the alchemy of myth-making: it takes disparate sources of prestige and merges them into one story. The Brutus myth thereby established a royal genealogy for Britain that was second to none – as old as any people on earth, and touched by the divine. This genealogy not only flattered British self-image but also provided a moral template: as the descendants of noble Trojans, the Britons should live up to that heritage; as beneficiaries of Diana's prophecy, they had a duty to maintain the sanctity of the land granted to them. These ideas would echo down the centuries whenever leaders sought to invoke the ancient past for authority or inspiration.

Druidic Lore and Spiritual Themes in the Brutus Legend

Though the story of Brutus is rooted in classical myth, it did not remain purely secular in its interpretation. Over time, spiritual and "druidic" dimensions were read into the legend, blending it with the mystical heritage of the Celts and the concept of sacred kingship.

In Brutus's tale we find a striking scene of divine revelation: the episode of the Temple of Diana. Here is a Trojan hero, performing a ritual sacrifice and praying in an abandoned shrine, who then receives a dream-message from a goddess. This has a spiritual resonance that later ages would not overlook. To medieval Christian writers, Diana's prophecy could be seen allegorically – perhaps as a manifestation of God's will (with Diana merely the vessel). To neo-pagans and romantics of much later times, this scene was positively druidic in flavour: a hero communing with a deity in a sacred grove or temple under the night sky, guided by visions. In the 18th and 19th centuries, when Britain experienced a revival of interest in Druidism, some drew parallels between Brutus's oracle and the ancient Celtic seers. They imagined that Britain's destiny was foretold not only by a Roman goddess but in the stars and landscapes revered by Druids.

While the original chronicles do not mention Druids in Brutus's time (Druids appear later in the stories of Celtic Britain, around the time of the Roman conquest), later writers loved to retroject spiritual significance back onto Brutus's arrival. The idea emerged that Albion was a sacred land even before Brutus, perhaps known to ancient sages. Some 17th-century antiquarians speculated that Eastern patriarchs or priests might have visited the isle in prehistoric times. There were fanciful theories that Trojan refugees could have brought esoteric wisdom or Eastern religious practices with them. A few even suggested that the Druids themselves might have been influenced by or descended from Trojan priests who came with Brutus. Such notions are not historically supported, but they show an attempt to connect Britain's spiritual heritage (Druidic Celtic religion) with the Brutus myth. If the Britons came from the classical world, could their religion (Druidism) have roots there too? Perhaps the Trojans encountered ancient wisdom traditions during their wanderings – so the thinking went – and transplanted them to Albion's shores along with everything else.

What we can say more concretely is that the legend of Brutus does carry a sacred kingship motif. Brutus isn't just a conqueror; he is a lawgiver and nation-founder. Geoffrey of Monmouth portrays Brutus as creating laws for the Britons after founding New Troy. This mirrors how Moses delivered laws to the Israelites, or how legendary kings like Minos or Lycurgus gave laws in Greek tradition. It implies that Brutus was not only the physical progenitor but also the spiritual father of the nation, setting the moral and legal order. This feeds into the later concept of British kingship being sanctified by ancient tradition. Medieval Welsh writers, for example, often referred to "the laws of Dyfnwal Moelmud" – supposedly ancient British laws from a successor of Brutus – to assert that Britain had lawgivers long before the Romans. Brutus's role as first lawmaker gave subsequent kings a kind of ancestral authority to invoke.

Another spiritual aspect is the idea of Britain as a promised land. Diana's prophecy clearly casts Albion in that light: a prepared place, rich and awaiting Brutus's people. This has echoes of the Israelites' promise of Canaan. In later centuries, some British writers likened their island to a new

Canaan or Zion, chosen by God. The Arthurian legends – themselves an outgrowth of the Brutus narrative – often imbued Britain with a mystical quality (the Quest for the Holy Grail, for example, treats the land as holy ground that must remain pure for the holy relic to be found). In those Arthurian tales, the health of the kingdom is tied to the virtue of the king (the Fisher King motif). We can trace a faint line back from that idea to Brutus: as the first king granted the land by divine sanction, one could imagine that if Brutus had failed in virtue, the blessing might not have held. Fortunately, Brutus is depicted as a noble and just figure, so the land prospers under him. The concept of sacred geography takes root here – the land of Albion itself is portrayed almost as a character, with a fate and fortune linked to the moral order established by its first ruler.

Albion as sacred geography also found expression in Renaissance works like Michael Drayton's *Poly-Olbion* (1612). *Poly-Olbion* is essentially a poetic chorography, where rivers, hills, and plains of England and Wales are personified and speak. In its frontispiece, *Albion* (as a female figure) sits enthroned, and around her are images of legendary figures including Brutus. Drayton, while focusing on landscape, doesn't forget the mythic founders – he invokes Brutus early as the one who gave the land its name and initial story. The very title *Poly-Olbion* means "Very Albion" or "abundantly Albion", indicating an exploration of the mythic essence of the land. This poem, like others of its era, treats Albion as a land with almost spiritual personality, whose rivers might remember the coming of Brutus and whose hills might still echo with the footsteps of giants. Such imaginative works reinforced the notion that every corner of the island was touched by myth – that geography and legend were inseparable in Britain.

Now, if we consider Druids specifically: by Roman accounts, Druids were the priestly caste among the Celtic Britons and Gauls, known for their wisdom, nature-worship, and possibly human sacrifice. They came to symbolise ancient arcane knowledge in later imagination. While Druids aren't contemporaries of Brutus in the story (since Brutus's tale predates the Iron Age Celtic culture), some Victorian and modern neo-druidic thinkers embraced Brutus as part of their mythos. For example, Iolo Morganwg (Edward Williams), an 18th-century Welsh antiquarian who helped revive modern Druidism, was known to incorporate various British legends (though he forged some of his "triads"). It's not a stretch to think he would have gladly tied Druidic lineage to Brutus's Trojan refugees if it served to legitimise Britain's ancient wisdom. The logic would be: Brutus's people settled Britain and over generations became the Celtic Britons; their priests and wise men eventually were known as Druids. Therefore, the line of wisdom goes back to the classical world. Even some earlier scholars like John Aubrey (17th c.) and William Stukeley (18th c.) speculated on druidic connections to eastern mysteries – Stukeley at one point suggested Druids were heirs to the patriarchal religion (even linking them vaguely to Abraham). While these were not directly about Brutus, they contributed to an intellectual atmosphere where mythic history and spiritual identity were interwoven.

One concrete example of spiritual overlay is the legend that Joseph of Arimathea came to Britain, bringing the Holy Grail to Glastonbury. Though separate from Brutus's tale, this Christian legend of Britain's sanctification complements the Brutus myth. Together they suggest that Britain was both classically ordained (by Brutus's Trojans) and Christianly ordained (by Joseph and later by conversion of the kings) to be a sacred isle. In an almost poetic way, one could say Brutus prepared the land for the eventual coming of Christianity; he laid the foundations of a kingdom that would one day become the first Christian empire under Constantine (born in Britain, according to legend) and later a cradle of reformed Christianity. Some Arthurian stories even have an endpoint where Arthur's lineage from Brutus converges with the spiritual mission of the Grail, fusing the two threads.

Thus, spiritually, Brutus's story was sometimes read as an allegory of divine providence: the Trojan escape signifying survival by grace, the prophecy signifying divine guidance, the victory over giants symbolising triumph over chaos, and the founding of a just nation prefiguring the establishment of a godly kingdom. It gave the British a sense that their realm was under a special mandate. Kings, in particular, liked this idea. The notion of *sacred kingship* – that a monarch isn't just a secular ruler but has a quasi-religious role as the guardian of his people's fate and the land's fertility – found fuel in legends like Brutus. Early modern kings, as we'll see, would capitalise on that.

In summary, while Brutus's tale began as a pagan heroic saga, it accrued spiritual significance and druidic romance over the centuries. Albion, the stage of his exploits, came to be seen as a land destined not only for worldly glory but for spiritual importance. The myth bridged the gap between Britain's pre-Christian Celtic identity (with Druids and nature reverence) and its classical identity (with Trojan and Roman connections). Later poets and mystics could thus claim Brutus as a hero of both sword and soul – a conduit through which the divine purpose for Albion was first made manifest. In this way, the legend contributed to a sense of Britain as "homeland of ancient wisdom": whether that wisdom was druidic lore, the light of Grail Christianity, or the enlightened rule of lawful kings, it all had its deep roots in the mythic soil first tilled by Brutus and his followers on their arrival in blessed Albion.

Medieval Chroniclers and the Legacy of the "Brut"

To understand how the Brutus legend shaped British identity, one must see how thoroughly it permeated medieval historical writing. From the 12th century onward, the story of Brutus became almost canonical in British historiography – to the point that medieval Britons regarded Brutus as a factual figure, the way we consider, say, King Alfred or William the Conqueror. This was largely thanks to the influence of key chroniclers and the propagation of the tale in multiple languages.

The earliest extant mention of Brutus by name comes from the *Historia Brittonum* (c. 829, often attributed to Nennius). In it, after listing various descendants of Noah, the compiler introduces Brutus as a descendant of Aeneas who eventually reached Britain. The account is brief, but it sets the foundation: Britain is named for Brutus, who filled it with his descendants, we are told. It's clear that by Nennius's time, there was an existing oral or written tradition linking the Britons to Troy. Some scholars think this tradition might have been influenced by similar origin myths circulating in Europe – for example, the Franks had a legend that they were descended from Francus, a survivor of Troy, and the Romans had the Aeneid. Isidore of Seville (7th c.) even speculated that the name "Britain" came from *bruti* (brutes), but this was a pun rather than a lineage. Nennius's account attempts more: it ties Brutus into the biblical chronology and gives a semblance of history.

But the true explosion of the Brutus story came with Geoffrey of Monmouth. Around 1136, Geoffrey completed his *Historia Regum Britanniae* ("History of the Kings of Britain"), a sweeping pseudo-historical account of the Britons from the Trojan days up to the 7th century. Geoffrey devotes the opening chapters to Brutus, greatly expanding the narrative with rich detail (much of which we've recounted earlier: the prophecy of Diana, the battles with Pandrasus, detour in Gaul, etc.). Geoffrey's work was a medieval bestseller. It spread across Europe; by the end of the 12th century there were translations and adaptations in various tongues. It's Geoffrey who firmly entrenched Brutus in the national story of Britain. After him, virtually every chronicle of British history – whether written in Latin, French, or English – started with Brutus's arrival or at least acknowledged it.

One of the first adaptations was by Wace, a Norman poet, who in 1155 rendered Geoffrey's Latin into Anglo-Norman French verse. His work, called *Roman de Brut*, made the story accessible to the Anglo-Norman aristocracy (who spoke French). Wace kept the core elements and added a few embellishments of his own. Notably, he popularized certain names and episodes in a more chivalric tone.

Soon after, around 1190–1200, an English priest named Layamon composed Brut, one of the earliest lengthy poems in the Middle English language (and indeed, one of the first major works of English literature post-Conquest). Layamon explicitly says he took inspiration from Wace and "an English book" (possibly a West English version of the story). Layamon's *Brut* is over 16,000 lines long – an enormous undertaking – and it covers the history of Britain from the Trojan war and the fall of Troy all the way to the founding of Britain by Brutus, and onward through centuries to the Saxon times. The fact that Layamon, writing in the English of the West Midlands, chose to retell this entire saga shows how deeply the Brutus narrative had penetrated even regions far from the Norman court. His audience likely included local gentry or monastic readers who wanted an English account of their land's history. By calling his work *Brut*, Layamon centers Brutus as the key figure (the title essentially means "History of Brutus/Britain"). It speaks volumes that Britain's history was often simply referred to as *"The Brut"* – as if Brutus encapsulated it all. "The Brut" became a synonym for the chronicle of British kings.

Throughout the 13th and 14th centuries, many other chronicles – in Latin and in the developing vernaculars (Middle English, Welsh) – reproduced Geoffrey's narrative. There are multiple Middle English prose chronicles known as *Bruts* that start with Brutus. In Wales, Geoffrey's work was translated into Welsh as *Brut y Brenhinedd* (Chronicle of the Kings) and it influenced Welsh historical memory profoundly. The Welsh were proud to trace themselves to Bryttan / Prydain, eponymous founder (Brutus). In their triads and genealogies, they enumerate the line of kings from Brutus down to Cadwaladr, etc.

This widespread retelling meant that generation upon generation of Britons (especially those of the educated class) grew up believing Britain had a Trojan origin story. It was taught almost as conventional history. Monks in monasteries copied these works, sometimes illustrating them. The story of Brutus, of the giants, of King Locrine, Queen Cordelia (Lear's daughter, also from Geoffrey) and the others, all became part of the national lore. It's no coincidence that even centuries later, writers like Shakespeare tapped into this pool (Shakespeare's *King Lear* is ultimately drawn from Geoffrey's legendary kings, though Lear is much later than Brutus). The Matter of Britain, which includes the Brutus narrative and the Arthurian legend, stood alongside the Matter of Rome (classical heroes) and Matter of France (Charlemagne's paladins) as one of the three great cycles of medieval literature. It gave the British their own heroic saga to celebrate.

It's important to mention that not everyone accepted Geoffrey's account uncritically. Even in the 12th century, some scholars (especially outside Britain) were skeptical. The noted historian William of Newburgh (late 12th c.) famously dismissed Geoffrey's history as mostly fiction. However, such voices were drowned out by the romance of the story and the political utility it had. In the later Middle Ages, chroniclers like Ranulf Higden and Henry of Huntingdon did include the Brutus story, sometimes with caveats. But as time went on, more and more people in England and Wales took it for granted.

The impact on national identity was significant. By giving a common ancestor, Brutus provided a sense of unity. The Welsh, Cornish, and Brittonic people long considered themselves the true Britons (as opposed to the Saxon English). They held on to the Brutus myth as part of their heritage. When the Norman kings and later English kings realised the power of the legend, they co-opted it to legitimise their rule over all Britain. King Edward I, when conquering Wales in 1282, styled himself as the heir to the ancient British kings (and symbolically named his son Prince of Wales, assimilating that heritage). Chroniclers for Edward I tried to tie him to Arthur, and thus to Brutus. Similarly, Edward III, in claiming the throne of France, invoked the idea that as Britons (descended from Troy) the English might have an inherited claim equal or superior to the French (who traced themselves to Francus, another Trojan).

One sees the legend's political weight clearly in the Tudor period. The Tudors had Welsh blood (Henry VII descended from Welsh princes like Rhys ap Tewdwr). They actively embraced their Brittonic roots. Henry VII named his first son Arthur to evoke the legendary king and by extension Brutus's line. Though Prince Arthur died young, the symbolism was not lost: the Tudors were reviving the British line of kings. Under Henry VIII and Elizabeth I, the realm's propagandists promoted the idea of a "British Empire", meaning an empire that existed in antiquity (under Brutus and Arthur) before the Roman Empire reached Britain. When Henry VIII broke with the Pope, there was an effort to assert that English kings owed their authority to no outside power because they ruled by inheritance of Brutus's imperium. John Dee, advisor to Elizabeth I, explicitly used the term "British Empire" in 1576 and drew on historical precedents including Brutus to argue that the English monarch had a God-given imperial sway over the British Isles and beyond. This was part of a Renaissance concept of translatio imperii combined with national destiny.

However, the Tudor era also saw the first serious historical criticism of the Brutus myth. Polydore Vergil, an Italian humanist invited to England by Henry VII, wrote an *Anglica Historia* (1534) in which he openly questioned Geoffrey's fables. Polydore Vergil noted the lack of earlier evidence for Brutus and considered the story dubious. This angered some British antiquaries (a scholar named Leland defended the British chronicles vigorously). But Vergil's skepticism was a harbinger of the coming change: the rise of a more empirical approach to history in the 16th and 17th centuries.

Even so, popular and literary acceptance of Brutus remained high. Holinshed's Chronicles (1577 and 1587), which were a huge compendium of British history used by Shakespeare and others, begin with Albion, the giants, and Brutus – though Holinshed does present variant opinions (like those of John Bale and others on Neptune's sons), he still gives the legend a prominent place. This means that when Shakespeare was writing history plays, the context he had from Holinshed included these myths. In Shakespeare's Cymbeline, a play set in ancient Britain, there is a reference to the longstanding royal line and hints of Trojan origins. In King Lear, while the play doesn't mention Trojans, the source material in Geoffrey had Lear as a descendant of Brutus. The audience of the time, familiar with chronicles, would have known that backdrop.

Beyond chronicles, genealogical rolls and pageantry kept the Brutus tale alive. At the coronation of Elizabeth I (1559), pageant devices showed allegorical scenes of unity and antiquity. One pageant presented her lineage symbolically. And during James I's entry to London in 1604 as the new king of a united England and Scotland, one spectacle explicitly celebrated Albion and the line of Brutus culminating in James – positioning him as the restorer of the "ancient monarchy" of Britain. Poets addressed James as the heir of "Brute" and Arthur. In fact, James commissioned a new royal genealogy to be drawn up after he became king of *Great Britain*. Scholars like William Camden and John Speed worked on British histories that, while more cautious, still paid respect to the myth. One 17th-century pedigree by Owen Harry traced King James's ancestry "by divers direct lines to Brutus"– meaning they found multiple pathways through different medieval dynasties all the way back to the Trojan founder. This was plausible since many European noble lines claimed Trojan ancestry (through intermarriage, James could be connected via the Welsh princes, the Scottish kings, or even Continental houses that had their own Trojan legends).

In summary, medieval chroniclers established the Brutus narrative as the orthodox history of Britain, and this remained largely unchallenged in the popular imagination until the Enlightenment. It gave the British a rich store of heroes and episodes to draw national lessons from: Brutus exemplified leadership and daring; his great-grandson King Leir (Lear) exemplified folly in old age and the virtue of loyal children like Cordelia; Queen Cordelia herself (a mythical ruler in Geoffrey's account) exemplified wisdom and courage; and of course Arthur, descending from Brutus, became the paragon of kingship. The *Brut* tradition thus unified the legendary kings of Britain into one continuous saga, starting with a Trojan and ending with the last Briton king before the Saxons (often King Cadwaladr or King Arthur's exit). This saga was a source of pride and a wellspring for creative retellings. It was Britain's equivalent of the *Aeneid* or the *Nibelungenlied*, but with the unique twist that it pretended to be actual history.

The legacy of that in nation-building is immense. A people taught to believe their ancestors were epic heroes may feel a strong sense of collective worth. The medieval English and Welsh did, at times, unite under that banner – especially when facing outside threats. During the Hundred Years' War, for instance, English writers reminded people that Britons and Trojans defeated Greeks at Troy, so surely they could take on the French. Or, as in Drayton's poem mentioned, they imagined Albion surrounded by Brutus and other conquerors, implying the nation's invincibility through ages.

It's also telling that even after the medieval period, poets kept returning to the well of Brutus for inspiration. Spenser in the 1590s included an extensive allegorical history of Britain (Book II and III of *The Faerie Queene*), culminating explicitly with a Trojan origin of Britons and the line of kings through Brutus. Milton, in the 17th century, though skeptical, began his unpublished *History of Britain* with a summary of Brutus's tale, famously stating: "I might tell ye how Brutus...

according to the British fables... in the end wonne them this Iland" (he calls it a fable but still tells it because of its cultural importance).

Thus, through chroniclers and poets, the myth became memory. By around 1600, the average educated Englishman would know of Brutus of Troy as readily as an educated Greek knew of Hellen, the eponymous ancestor of the Hellenes. Only with the advent of more critical historiography in the late 17th and 18th centuries did the myth start to be treated overtly as non-factual. Yet even then, it persisted as a cherished legend if not literal truth.

Tudor and Stuart Visions: British Identity and Sacred Kingship Reborn

The Brutus myth provided abundant material for the Tudor and Stuart monarchs as they crafted ideologies of rule. In the 16th century, with the Wars of the Roses over and a new dynasty (the Tudors) on the throne, England was ripe for a unifying national story. The Tudors deftly used British myth – especially Arthurian and Brutan elements – to solidify their legitimacy and promote an image of historic destiny.

Henry VII, the first Tudor king, was of Welsh origin. The Welsh had long seen themselves as the direct descendants of the old Britons (Brutus's people) who had been displaced by the Anglo-Saxons. Henry's very rise to power was heralded in Welsh prophecies as the return of the Cymry (Britons) over the Saxons. After Henry won the crown in 1485, there was a clear effort to tie the Tudor lineage to Cadwaladr (a legendary last ancient British king) and through him back to Brutus. The idea was that Henry wasn't just another English king; he was reviving the line of Brutus that had been interrupted by the Norman Conquest. The publication of Sir Thomas Malory's

Le Morte d'Arthur by Caxton in 1485 – just after Henry's victory at Bosworth – is symbolic. Malory's compilation of Arthurian legend (which itself is an offshoot of Brutus's line) came out at precisely the time the new king was looking to Arthurian-British nostalgia to shore up support. Indeed, Henry VII's choice to name his heir "Arthur" was a deliberate piece of this myth making. Had Prince Arthur lived and become king, the Arthurian connection would have been trumpeted even more.

Under Henry VIII, and especially after he established the Church of England separate from Rome, the notion of England (or Britain) as an empire unto itself gained prominence. Parliament's Act of Appeals in 1533 declared that *"this realm of England is an Empire"* governed by one supreme head (the king) – implying it owed no allegiance to external authorities like the Pope or Holy Roman Emperor. The conceptual background for calling England an *Empire* drew in part on the ancient idea of a British empire under Brutus and Arthur. Scholars at Henry's court emphasized that English kings had from time immemorial been "Emperors" in their own dominions, citing how Brutus was an independent monarch who predated Rome's influence. Some writers contrasted the British Empire of Brutus with the Roman Empire, arguing that the former was revived under the Tudors to challenge the latter's successor (the Habsburg Holy Roman Empire and Papal power). This played well into the politics of the day, as Henry VIII and later Elizabeth positioned themselves against Catholic powers.

Elizabeth I's reign (1558–1603) saw a flourish of English national self-confidence. Though Elizabeth herself was cautious about explicitly claiming descent from Brutus (she was childless and perhaps less keen to push a lineage theme), the arts and literature of her time fully embraced Britannic myth. Edmund Spenser's *Faerie Queene* is a prime example. In Book III, canto 9, Spenser presents a pageant of famous Britons: he mentions "Troynovant" (London) and recounts how Brutus, a Trojan, conquered the natives and founded Britain. He does this to set the stage for celebrating Queen Elizabeth's lineage as part of that grand continuum (implicitly, she inherits the throne that began with Brutus and was made glorious by Arthur). The very concept of the Virgin Queen ruling a land favored by providence ties back to the old myths – Elizabeth was often depicted as Diana or Cynthia (moon goddess) in court masques, interestingly the same goddess who guided Brutus.

Elizabeth's astrologer advisor John Dee went even further. In his writings on empire (like the 1577 *General and Rare Memorials*), Dee asserts England's sovereign claim over the seas and newly discovered lands by linking it to an ancient precedent. He referenced Geoffrey's history to argue that the British were always a seafaring, imperial people since Brutus's time. Dee also popularized the term "British Empire," consciously invoking Brutus (a Briton) as the first emperor of the isle. This helped build ideological groundwork for English claims in the New World, by suggesting that expansion was a return to ancient greatness.

Now, the Stuarts (starting with James I in 1603) had the unique position of ruling both England and Scotland, effectively reuniting much of "Albion." James was very keen on the idea of a single kingdom of "Great Britain." He often invoked the term and even had coins minted with the name *Britannia.* The Brutus legend was a convenient unifier: recall that Brutus's three sons Locrinus, Albanactus, and Kamber were said to have divided the island into Loegria (England), Albania (Scotland), and Kambria (Wales). So all these regions had a shared father. James I used this myth to present himself as the heir to that original unity – essentially, as a new Brutus reuniting his children's realms. In 1604, when he assumed the title "King of Great Britain," some of his supporters traced the idea back to Brutus's time as the last moment the isle was truly unified under one crown. Writers noted that the precedents for a King of Great Britain were Brutus (the first king to rule the whole isle) and King Egbert in the 9th century (who had titled himself Bretwalda or "Britain-ruler"). By citing Brutus and Egbert, James's propagandists gave historical weight to his union of crowns. One genealogist even connected James to both Brutus and Egbert in lineage, as if to say he had a double right to rule a united Britain. During James's reign and that of his son Charles I, masques and literary works continued to reference Albion and Trojan origins. For instance, Ben Jonson wrote a masque for James's queen, Anne of Denmark, called *The Masque of Albion* (1608), which involved personifications of the rivers of Britain welcoming the King and Queen as new rulers of Albion's land. In another performance for Prince Henry (James's eldest son), Jonson presented "Prince Henry as the embodiment of Arthur, inheritor of Trojan-British glory." The Stuart court loved such classical allusions. When Charles I was crowned in 1625, poets again reached for ancient British themes to bless the new king.

However, we should note a growing dichotomy: the learned antiquaries of the late 16th and 17th century were increasingly doubting the historicity of Brutus. William Camden in his *Britannia* (1586) expresses measured skepticism about the Trojan claims, though he recounts them. By the time of the English Civil War (1640s), some scholars outright labeled Brutus a fable. Yet, simultaneously, the monarchy (especially when struggling, like during the Stuart period) leaned on these old symbols for legitimacy. It's telling that after the monarchy was restored in 1660, one of the entertainments commissioned was *"Albion Restored"*. Even as late as the 18th century, the legend had its believers: the poet James Thomson, in his poem *"Rule, Britannia!"* (1740), speaks of Britons never being slaves, possibly alluding to an inherent freedom dating back to their Trojan forefathers who liberated themselves and found a free land.

One fascinating expression of the enduring myth in civic life was the tradition of the Guildhall Giants in London. Since at least Henry V's time (early 15th century), the city of London has paraded large effigies of Gog and Magog (the giant guardians) in the annual Lord Mayor's Show. These giants in popular lore came to be identified with the last giants defeated by Brutus's Trojans. Thus, even in the pageantry of the capital, the memory of Brutus's conquest was kept alive year after year: Gog and Magog were symbolically chained or subservient, "guarding" the City of London, as if acknowledging Brutus's victory. As the official Lord Mayor's Show website notes, *"They are Gog and Magog, traditional guardians of the City, carried in the Lord Mayor's Show since the reign of Henry V"*. So a direct line runs from myth to civic ritual: Londoners celebrating their mythic origins through these figures.

Under the Tudors and Stuarts, therefore, the story of Brutus influenced both high politics and popular culture. It gave monarchs a theme of sacred kingship – the king as heir of a line ordained by the gods and sanctified by antiquity. Early Stuart masques often portrayed the king as a bringer of harmony to Albion, much like Brutus brought order to a wild land. The idea that the monarch's reign was the fulfillment of ancient prophecy (Diana's or otherwise) was a flattering one. For example, when James I made peace and united the crowns, some poets mused that *Diana's prophecy to Brutus* had hinted not only at Brutus's own time but at a future reconciliation of Albion's divided kingdoms under one ruler (James himself).

The Tudors, claiming Arthurian descent, and the Stuarts, championing British union, both found Brutus useful as an archetype. Even during the tumultuous 17th century, Royalists occasionally invoked the ancient constitution of Britain (which included the idea of kingship beginning with Brute) to argue against Parliament's claims in the civil war. After the Glorious Revolution of 1688, more rational minds like Bishop Gilbert Burnet would ridicule the old Trojan myth, but it lingered in education and lore.

By 1700, though erudite opinion had turned against the literal truth of Brutus, the symbolic power of the myth was entrenched. Britain (now formally Great Britain after 1707 with the union of England and Scotland) was often personified as "Albion" or "Britannia" – poetic names that harken back to the island's oldest known monikers. The union flag of the UK is sometimes nicknamed "Brunion Jack" in jest (not a historical term, but playing on union and Brutus). More seriously, 18th-century unionist tracts occasionally referenced that England and Scotland were "two sons of Brutus" reunited under Queen Anne or the Hanoverians.

In conclusion, the Tudor and early Stuart periods represent the zenith of conscious use of the Brutus myth for statecraft. British identity was explicitly built around it – historians of that era have observed that *"During the middle ages a British identity was developed around the legendary figure of Brutus of Troy"*, and the Tudors in particular *"consolidated a British identity around their rule"*. This British identity, rooted in ancient tradition, became a vehicle for political ambition: it underpinned the vision of an empire and the challenge to European rivals. By linking themselves to

Brutus, the monarchs of a small island kingdom could stand tall among emperors, claiming a pedigree as old and esteemed as any on earth. This shows the enduring allure of the myth: long after its factual credibility waned, it continued to provide inspiration, cohesion, and a sense of destiny to the people of Britain."

Albion as a Mythic and Sacred Geography

Throughout the evolving legend of Brutus, the land of Albion (Britain) itself emerges not just as a backdrop, but as a character infused with mythic meaning. The concept of sacred geography refers to the idea that places and landscapes hold spiritual significance or are central to a people's mythic imagination. Albion, as the primal name of Britain, became exactly that – a landscape enlivened by legend, where every hill and river could be linked to ancient heroes or mystical events.

From the start, when Diana's prophecy guides Brutus, Albion is depicted as a blessed isle reserved by the gods. The notion that the island was *empty of mankind but full of promise* made it a sort of prelapsarian paradise, *terra nullius* gifted to Brutus's people. This naturally invites comparison to other mythical lands: Atlantis, perhaps, or the Biblical Eden, or the classical "Fortunate Isles". Indeed, later poets frequently called Britain a *Fortunate Isle*, echoing this idea of a westward paradise. The prophecy frames Albion as destiny's arena, a virgin land waiting for its destined inhabitants. That planted the seed of an enduring belief: that Britain holds a special place in the divine scheme.

As medieval writers fleshed out the geography of Geoffrey's account, they tied many locations to the Brutus narrative. We have noted a few already: Totnes in Devon with the Brutus Stone where he supposedly landed; London (Troynovant) said to be founded by Brutus; the cliff in Cornwall (near Plymouth) from which Corineus hurled Gogmagog, known in folklore as Giant's Leap or Lam Goemagot. Such toponyms and local legends anchored the national myth in real soil and stone.

London, especially, gained a quasi-sacred status thanks to its mythical foundation. Medieval Londoners proudly embraced the name Troynovaunt or Trinovantum, a corruption which Geoffrey explained as deriving from New Troy. They believed their city was as ancient as Rome, founded by a hero of equal stature. A curious legend arose that Ludgate (one of London's gates) was named after King Lud, a supposed descendant of Brutus, and that Lud was buried near that gate and had reigned in Troynovant. Lud's two sons, Androgeus and Tenvantius, were said to be the source of the name *Trinovantum* (a delightful etymological fancy). At St. Paul's Cathedral, longtime rumor held that it stood on the site of Brutus's Temple of Diana, and the London Stone embedded in Cannon Street was thought to be a relic of that temple's altar. As one Victorian saying went, "So long as the Stone of Brutus is safe, so long shall London flourish."

Here we see how a piece of geology (the London Stone) became sacralized by the myth. The stone was first recorded in the 10th century as a landmark; by the 19th century it had the legendary attribution to Brutus. Londoners thus walked daily past a supposed talisman of their city's mythical origin – a direct link to Brutus ensuring the city's prosperity. Outside London, many other sites took on legendary associations. Geoffrey mentioned Brutus founding Troia Nova on the Thames, but he didn't detail other town foundings except Tours in Gaul. Later chroniclers and local traditions filled in

49

gaps: places like Totnes (as discussed), Dartmoor or Gogmagog Hills near Cambridge (named after giants, though likely from later tales), and Caer Troia (an old Welsh name for London). In Wales, the very name for Britain in Welsh, *Prydain*, comes from Bryttania (Brutus's Britain). Welsh legend had a notion of "Ynis Prydein" (the Isle of Britain) which was central to their prophetic literature. One famous collection, the *Triads of the Island of Britain*, often alludes to events "before the *corani* (Saxons) came" when the Island of Britain was ruled by the race of the Cymry (Britons). The triads list mythic events on the island, some involving figures from Geoffrey's history, thus merging local lore with the Brutus narrative.

Another myth to explain Albion's name (besides Albina's) was that the island was called Albion due to its *white* cliffs (Latin *albus* = white). This more prosaic explanation was known since Roman times (Pliny and others mention the white cliffs and the name Albion). But Geoffrey's storyline conveniently allowed both: originally Albion (maybe from a giant's name or white cliffs), then changed to Britannia after Brutus. Some Renaissance antiquaries tried to sort out these layered names. Camden, for instance, acknowledged the white cliffs origin but also recounted the Albina tale as folklore. Regardless of etymology, the persistent use of "Albion" in poetry kept alive a sense of antiquity. "Albion" as a poetic term for Britain became especially popular in the 16th–18th centuries. Spenser, Milton, Blake – all used Albion when they wanted to evoke a primal, ideal image of the nation. Milton in his *Hymn on the Nativity* (1629) references "the Lion and **old Albion" to symbolize England. Blake went even further, making Albion a character, the primeval man representing humanity (and specifically the people of Britain) in his complex mythopoeia. In Blake's lore, Albion is a giant who falls and must be regenerated – a potent metaphor using the country's name as an allegory for the soul of man.

If we consider sacred geography in a literal spiritual sense, one might think of ley lines or mystical alignments of ancient sites. In the 20th century, some enthusiasts (like Alfred Watkins, who coined "ley lines") thought ancient Britons laid out their sacred sites in straight lines across the landscape. They sometimes referenced myths to bolster the mysterious significance of these sites. While this is far removed from medieval legends, it's part of the long tail of treating Albion as *not just dirt and rock, but hallowed ground*. The proliferation of stone circles, barrows, and druidic lore in Britain certainly contributed to the atmosphere in which a legend like Brutus's could thrive. People saw Stonehenge, the White Horse of Uffington, the giant effigies on hillsides, and without scientific dating, they integrated them into the mythic timeline. Geoffrey's history even tries to account for Stonehenge (though attributing it to Merlin in the time of Aurelius Ambrosius). So the physical landscape of Britain was constantly read through a mythic lens.

During the romantic era, writers like Wordsworth and Coleridge visited sites like Tintern Abbey or remote Scottish glens and felt a deep spiritual presence, though they didn't directly invoke Brutus. But William Blake explicitly returns to Albion. In one of his famous images, *Glad Day or The Dance of Albion*, Blake depicts a joyous naked figure (the primordial Albion) with arms outstretched, symbolising freedom and spiritual awakening. To Blake, Albion represented England's spiritual identity – which had become shackled by industrialisation and materialism and needed liberation. Blake was certainly aware of the old legends; he even wrote a poetic line "All things begin and end in Albion's ancient Druid rocky shore." Here he conflates the ideas of Albion, Brutus's land, with Druids and an eternal cycle. Blake's prophecies imagine a New Jerusalem being built in England's green and pleasant land – another instance of seeing Britain as sacred space (drawing from the legend that Joseph of Arimathea brought the Gospel to Glastonbury).

In the 19th century, as modern archaeology began, belief in Brutus as a real person vanished among scholars. Yet the cultural motifs persisted. The Victorians loved King Arthur (Tennyson's *Idylls of the King* was immensely popular). With Arthur comes inevitably the backdrop of Brutus, though Victorian retellings often started the story with Arthur's immediate ancestors and glossed over Brutus in a few sentences. Still, Victorian medievalists and painters (like the Pre-Raphaelites) sometimes depicted scenes of ancient Britain: for example, John Martin, a painter known for biblical epics, also painted *"The Bard"* showing a lone Druid on a cliff as Edward I's army invades – tying historical events to mythic imagery of Druids in the landscape of Albion.

It's also worth noting that scientific geography sometimes humorously intersected with the legend. When geology in the 19th century proved Britain was once connected to the continent, the term "Albion" (which some had linked to a giant or to a daughter of Neptune) took on a new connotation: "Albion's severing from Gaul" became a phrase in geological discussions. Some scholars playfully said perhaps that was the flood that let Brutus arrive just in time to find an empty land. Of course, this was not serious; by then people treated Brutus as myth. But it shows how ingrained in the lexicon these mythic references were – even men of science named the hypothetical ancient land bridging England and France "Lyonesse" or other legendary names.

In the present day, Albion and Brutus still appear in literature and popular references. Modern fantasy novels or alternative histories sometimes revive the Trojan settlement idea. The myth remains a source of creative inspiration precisely because it casts Britain in an epic light. For example, some contemporary fiction posits "what if the Trojan origin were true?" or integrates it into fantasy worlds.

On the ground, many places in Britain quietly commemorate the myth. In Totnes, aside from the Brutus Stone on the high street, there are occasional re-enactments or children's stories about the landing. In London Guildhall, two large wooden statues of Gog and Magog stand (carved in the 1950s to replace ones destroyed in WWII) as the traditional guardians – with plaques explaining their legendary origin with Brutus. Thus even tourists encounter vestiges of the legend.

Finally, the concept of Britain as a "sacred geography" resonates strongly in neo-pagan and New Age circles today. Modern Druids (such as the Order of Bards, Ovates and Druids) frequently hold ceremonies at ancient sites like Stonehenge or Avebury, invoking the spirit of the land and often referencing "the ancestors of this island". While they may not mention Brutus by name (since he's not a Celtic figure), they speak of Albion as a living entity – a direct inheritance of the mythic view fostered over centuries. The poetic name "Albion" is used in rituals to mean the spiritual landscape of Britain.

In summary, Albion as a place became enshrined in myth: first as the land gifted to Brutus, later as a realm of wonder where giants roamed, then as a unified kingdom of Britons, and eventually as a symbol of Britain's enduring spirit. The mythic mapping of Britain – overlaying the physical map with legendary landmarks and stories – helped people in every era find meaning in their surroundings. A hill was not just a hill; it might be where a giant fell. A stone was not just a stone; it might be where the founder stepped ashore. This sacralisation of geography strengthened national identity: it's easier to love your land if every feature has a heroic tale. It also gave a sense that the very earth of Britain was charged with destiny. As a Victorian writer once put it, "**There's not a mete of English ground, betwixt the four seas, but was some time or other dear to hearts long since, and Albion herself doth keep their ancient memory." In the saga of Brutus, land and legend merged to create an Albion that is as much an idea as a place – an archetype of the beloved homeland, rich with echoes of a mythic past.

Legacy: The Enduring Echoes of Brutus and Albion

The legend of Brutus and the land of Albion, though long discredited as literal history, has left an indelible imprint on British cultural memory and identity. Over more than a millennium, it transformed and adapted, finding new relevance in each age – from monastic chronicle to courtly romance to national propaganda to poetic myth. What began as a creative attempt by medieval scribes to fill a historical void ended up shaping how a people understood themselves in relation to the ancient world and the divine.

By the eighteenth century, academic historians like Edward Gibbon or David Hume paid little heed to Brutus except as a quaint fable. Modern archaeology and history have shown that Britain's population emerged from waves of prehistoric migration quite unrelated to Trojans. Yet, the value of the Brutus narrative was never really in factual data; it was in the *story*. And stories, especially founding myths, have their own truth – a cultural or moral truth that resonates beyond fact. In this case, the truth it carried was the notion that nations need origins that speak to their character and aspirations. For medieval Britons, being children of Troy gave them dignity and destiny. For Renaissance Britons, it gave them unity and imperial ambition. For Romantics, Albion gave them spiritual depth and poetic muse.

Even today, threads of the legend persist in language and symbolism. Britannia, the female personification of Britain (seen on coins and statues), holds a trident and shield – symbols connecting her to both Neptune (sea power) and ancient warrior heritage. Though Britannia as an icon came via Roman influence, her name is the Latin for "land of Britons" (from Brutus/Britto). The very idea of Britannia ruling the waves might be said to hark back to the myth that Neptune's son Albion once ruled the seas and that Brutus arrived by divine guidance across the waves.

In British literature classes, students still encounter references that require knowledge of the Trojan-Briton connection: Milton's mention of *"Troynovant"*, Pope's satiric jibe in *The Dunciad* about "Brute" founding Britain, or even Joyce's use of "proud Albion" in *Ulysses*. The name "New Troy" was sometimes poetically given to London into the 19th century. A London newspaper in the 1800s was titled The Albion, assuming readers would get the allusion. And of course, in the realm of fantasy, modern authors occasionally reimagine the Brutus tale – for instance, in a speculative novel or game lore, one might find a storyline of refugees from a fallen empire colonising an island of giants (a clear echo of Brutus).

One might ask: what psychological need did the Brutus and Albion story fulfil for the British? On one level, it was the need for antiquity and prestige – no nation in Europe wanted to appear "new" or upstart; linking to Troy, the oldest epic saga, conferred grandeur. On another level, it was the need for cohesion – a myth that could be shared by the diverse peoples of the British Isles, giving them a common ancestor and narrative (despite internal conflicts, this remained a unifying backbone in concept). On a spiritual level, it satisfied the need to see one's homeland as blessed or chosen – to believe there is meaning in one's national story, that one's forebears were guided by fate or divine providence. That instills pride and perhaps a sense of responsibility.

Over time, of course, British identity and statecraft moved on to other frameworks (the influence of Enlightenment thought, then industrial and colonial narratives, etc.). Yet, intriguingly, even the British Empire at its height was often justified in quasi-mythic terms: the Victorians spoke of a civilising mission and occasionally likened themselves to Romans and, implicitly, to those ancient Trojans from whom they once claimed descent. And in the 20th century, during Britain's darkest hours in World War II, Winston Churchill famously invoked Britain's ancient spirit and island defiance – indirectly reminiscent of the old concept of a sea-girt Albion standing strong as destiny's people. It's as if these myths, though not explicitly cited, had seeped into the national subconscious.

In the realm of modern spirituality and neo-romanticism, as mentioned, William Blake's Albion has had a revival among those who read his prophecies as guidance for personal or national renewal. In Blake's mythology, the Giant Albion's fall and resurrection symbolise England's fall into materialism and hoped-for rebirth into a nation of imagination and brotherhood. This is a far cry from Brutus slaying giants, yet Blake chose the name Albion deliberately – tying his visionary tale back to the mythic name of the land. It shows that even when the specifics of Brutus were no longer tenable, the symbolic framework he inhabited (Albion as a special land, the British as an ancient people) remained potent.

To illustrate the surprising persistence of the legend's elements: In 1997, during the debate over Scottish devolution, one journalist whimsically referred to the event as "Albanactus reclaiming his heritage," alluding to the son of Brutus who took Albany (Scotland). And when the 2012 London Olympics opening ceremony took place, the producers included the Gogmagog giants as massive puppets in the spectacle, nodding to British folklore – a wink that only those familiar with London tradition and myth would fully get.

Thus, the echoes of Brutus and Albion are subtle but present in British cultural consciousness. They have transcended their origin in Geoffrey's medieval romantic history and become archetypal. Brutus stands as the archetype of the founder – bold, adventurous, claiming a new world. Albion stands as the archetype of the cherished homeland – ancient, beautiful, worth fighting for and preserving.

We began with Brutus setting sail from a fallen Troy, guided by a vision of Albion. In a way, this mirrors Britain's own continuous rebirth: from the fall of Roman Britain came the vision of an independent Britonnic kingdom under figures like Arthur; from the fall of medieval independence to Norman rule came the vision of a blended Anglo-British kingdom under the Plantagenets and Tudors; from the loss of the American colonies came a renewed vision of a more just and reformed British society at home; from the decline of empire came a vision of a "New Jerusalem" of social welfare (indeed Churchill during WWII referenced Blake's *Jerusalem* hymn). The pattern of something old falling and a new hope arising is embedded in that founding myth – the Trojans lost their city but founded a new one in a promised land. It's a narrative of resilience and renewal that can inspire any generation.

In closing, the history of Brutus and the land of Albion is a testament to the power of myth in shaping reality. While Brutus the man may never have existed, Brutus the idea helped forge a very real British identity. Albion, the geological island, may date back billions of years, but Albion the sacred isle gave countless inhabitants a reason to love and mythologize their home. The story provided meaning, continuity, and grandeur – things every nation's story strives for. And like all great stories, it could be retold and reinterpreted, from monkish Latin prose to troubadour's rhyme to renaissance masque to romantic poem, each time finding new life.

Today, standing atop the White Cliffs of Dover (the *alba* that likely gave Albion its name), one can gaze across the sea and reflect: somewhere beyond that horizon was Troy, the starting point of our mythic ancestor's voyage. Beneath our feet is Albion, the blessed soil he claimed. Of course, we know the story is legend – yet the very act of recalling it enriches our experience of this place. We sense the layers of human imagination that have consecrated the cliffs, the coasts, the hills with narrative. That is the true legacy of Brutus and Albion: they turned a mere stretch of earth into something legendary, a stage upon which generations have projected their highest ideals of heroism, unity, and destiny. And in doing so, they remind us that history is not only what happened, but also what we dream and believe about ourselves. Britain's dream, for a long and formative time, was Brutus's dream – of a new Troy flourishing in a green westward isle, an Albion eternal and blessed.

That dream, albeit now understood as myth, remains forever a part of the story of Britain. It lives on in the nation's poetry, its place-names, its symbols, and its collective subconscious – an immortal founding myth that, much like the Trojan War itself, will echo through the ages as long as tales of heroes and homelands are told.

The story of Brutus endured not because it was proven, but because it was believed. It gave a fractured land a common father. It gave kings their crowns and poets their metaphors. It filled the hollows of forgotten time with grandeur and hope.

Even today, the name Albion stirs something deeper than logic. It calls to the soul of the land. Whether Brutus was a man or a myth, he lives on in the names we still speak, the stones we still touch, and the stories we still tell.

He lives on in the dream of a better kingdom—one that remembers its sacred beginning.

Albion still dreams. And the story of Brutus is one of its oldest dreams.

A Mythic Invocation to the Reader

You who hold this book, you who hear the hush of these pages — listen. This is no ordinary tale, and these are no ordinary lands. You have been summoned not by chance but by the quiet pull of memory, something older than blood, older than language. The land itself has whispered to you.

It begins not in the mind, but in the bones — a stirring, a remembering. A sound beneath the soil, like breath moving through roots. The voice of Albion, long buried beneath layers of conquest and forgetting, begins to rise again, like morning mist from the fields of your ancestors.

You are not a stranger here.

You walk in the footprints of those who once called this island by names now half-lost to time — tribes who sang to the rivers and spoke with the stones, who read the skies not for war, but for guidance. You walk where the Durotriges lit fires on the hilltops, where the Regni told stories to the stars, where the Iceni, bold and unbroken, danced with their hare-footed goddess beneath the moon.

Their world is not dead. It is simply hidden. Waiting. Waiting for someone like you to turn aside from the noise of empire, to kneel in the soft earth, and remember.

In these pages, you will not find only history, but memory — the kind of memory that rises not through records, but through rivers, wind, and dream. The kind that clings to stone circles and ancient yews, that coils like the adder in tall grass, that croaks from the damp shadows with the toad, that blinks from the hedgerow with the hare, and cries from the sky with the hawk.

Each tribe, each path, each name you meet here carries more than information — it carries invitation. To remember who you are. To restore what has been lost. To return, not to a perfect past, but to a way of being in right relation with the land, with the unseen, and with each other.

This is a book of remembrance, of reweaving. A path not of nostalgia, but of awakening. The tribes of Britain were not only kin-groups and warriors — they were caretakers of mystery. Each people held a piece of the great pattern — not better, not worse, but necessary. The Belgae, the Dobunni, the Trinovantes — all flicker like constellations in the dark, each with a fire still burning, if only we learn again how to tend it.

So take these pages not only into your eyes, but into your breath. Light a candle. Touch the soil where you live. Speak the names aloud. And as you do, know that you are speaking with the land, not just about it.

You are walking with ancestors.

You are listening to the spirit of place.

You are answering the call that stirred Brutus from the shores of exile and drew the hare from Boudicca's chariot at the edge of battle. This is not merely a book. This is a threshold to Step through it.

CHAPTER 02

THE LEGACY OF BRUTUS AND THE TRIBAL SOUL OF ALBION

There is a moment in every great story where the myth begins to ripple outward into the real, like a stone cast into a still pond. The tale of Brutus, noble exile of Troy and first king of Albion, is not only a story of arrival or conquest — it is a story of transmission. Something ancient was handed down, not just through blood, but through the breath of the land, through dreams, through names spoken beside sacred fires.

To speak of the tribes of Britain without speaking of Brutus would be like trying to understand the roots of a tree without knowing the soil from which it grew.

Brutus did not merely found cities. He sowed the land with memory. Through his journey, his vision, and his blessing, the island came to be not simply inhabited, but awakened. And it was to the tribes that followed — the Dumnonii, the Durotriges, the Iceni and all their kin — that the task of keeping that memory alive was given.

When Brutus divided the land among his three sons — Locrinus, Kamber, and Albanactus — he did not simply grant them territories; he infused each region with a sacred charge. Loegria, Cambria, and Alba became not just places but principles. They held different *frequencies of the soul*, different moods of Albion. Each one carried a temperament, a guardianship, a purpose.

In time, these broader divisions gave rise to tribal configurations. The ancient memory, encoded in the land itself, began to fracture and diversify, like sunlight through leaves. Just as seeds from one plant may give rise to many different flowers, so too did Brutus's legacy give rise to many peoples. Each tribe held a part of the original dream. Each bore a sacred responsibility to their part of the land.

These weren't arbitrary boundaries drawn by politics or war — they were *land-bonded identities*. The Durotriges, with their hill forts, were perhaps the keepers of the old thresholds, guarding the inner mysteries of the south. The Dobunni, rooted near sacred springs and mists, may have watched over the soul of the water. The Iceni, proud and unyielding, stood as flame-bearers in the east. Each tribe sang a different note of Albion's ancient harmony.

And behind it all, as if just beneath the surface of consciousness, Brutus remained — not as a king on a throne, but as a kind of archetypal ancestor, the one who reminded all Britons that they were *called here, blessed here, planted here with purpose.*

It is no coincidence that so many tribes held kingship as a sacred trust. In tribal lore, a leader was more than a war-chief. He or she was often a spirit-link — a mediator between the land and the people. That idea was not born in a vacuum. It echoed the *first kingship*, the mythic kingship of Brutus, blessed by Diana and guided by vision.

Moreover, many tribes traced their lineages not just to human founders but to gods, animals, or elemental forces. The Cornovii, for example, were people of the horn — a potent symbol of divine power and protection. The Brigantes, dwellers of the highlands, took their name from a root meaning exalted or shining. These names suggest not only identity but initiation — an understanding that to belong to a tribe was to belong to something both ancestral and spiritual.

In this way, we begin to see the hidden thread. The tribes were not merely "post-Roman" or "Iron Age" political units, as modern classifications often reduce them. They were sacred stewards of an inherited mythos. Their stories, laws, songs, and borders were expressions of a deeper landscape — one carved as much by prophecy as by time.

The bardic traditions, too, helped to preserve this link. Across centuries, the keepers of lore remembered not only genealogies and battles, but the sacred meanings of places, of names, of rivers and hills. The land was alive with story. And at the root of many of those stories stood Brutus — not as a memory of conquest, but as a *symbol of belonging.* His tale gave the Britons a place in the great dance of world peoples — not as an afterthought of Rome or a footnote of empire, but as chosen by the gods, as the people of Albion.

This is the soul of tribal Britain — a soul formed not in isolation, but in mythic inheritance. To honour the tribes is to honour their myths. And to honour their myths is to remember Brutus, the dreamer who sailed beyond the world he knew to find a sleeping land — and wake it. In the chapters to come, we will dive into the names and symbols of each tribe. But let us never forget that behind each name, behind each banner, lies a thread of that first story — a thread that still winds its way through the rivers and ruins, through the stories whispered to children by firelight, and through the hearts of those who remember.

THE LEGACY OF BRUTUS
AND THE
TRIBAL SOUL OF ALBION

Albion did not forget her tribes. Nor should we.

CHAPTER 03

THE MEANING OF THE TRIBES — ETYMOLOGY AND SIGNIFICANCE OF TRIBAL NAMES

To understand the soul of a people, we must begin with their names.

The tribal names that once rang across the hills, rivers, and forests of ancient Britain were more than mere identifiers — they were sacred titles, spoken into being with intention and power. In their language lay echoes of their totems, their roles in the land, their spiritual relationships, and their worldviews. These names were not just spoken by the people — they were spoken by the land itself.

Each tribe's name carries the resonance of something essential — a gift, a challenge, a memory. Some point to animals and plants; others to divine ancestry, weapons, war cries, the spirit of place. When we speak these names aloud today, we're not just recounting history — we are rekindling a relationship, a sacred exchange with the past.

Let us journey through the etymology and meaning behind these ancient tribal names, and in doing so, illuminate the nature of their spirit, their story, and their sacred place upon the isle of Albion.

1. **Durotriges**
   Meaning: Possibly "fort dwellers" or "hillfort people" (from Celtic duro = fort + trig = inhabit) Significance: Known for their powerful hillforts, such as Maiden Castle, the Durotriges were deeply tied to the earthworks and sacred enclosures of the land. Their legacy echoes the importance of guardianship — they stood at the thresholds between tribe and wilderness, between safety and the unknown.

2. **Belgae**
   Meaning: Possibly from belg- meaning "to swell (with anger or courage)"
   Significance: A people of courage and boldness, the Belgae were known as fierce warriors and energetic settlers. Unlike older native tribes, they may have migrated from Gaul, bringing a different spiritual and martial edge. Their presence stirred the energies of Wessex and southern Britain.

3. **Regni (or Regnenses)**
   Meaning: Possibly "the royal ones" or "people of the ruler"

Significance: Tied to the southern coasts, the Regni were deeply associated with sovereignty, noble lineage, and alliance. Their name recalls ancient sacral kingship — that leadership must serve the land, not dominate it.

4. **Atrebates**
Meaning: Likely "dwellers" or "inhabitants" (from ad-treb — to settle, or home-place)
Significance: Grounded people, perhaps deeply tied to agricultural cycles and tribal kinship. Their sacred role was to hold space, to root, to tend.

5. **Dobunni**
Meaning: Possibly "people of the deep world" or "those of the dark places"
Significance: Thought to be peaceful and mystical, the Dobunni were associated with sacred waters, springs, and underground spaces. They may have been the spiritual caretakers of the land's hidden energy.

6. **Dumnonii**
Meaning: Possibly "people of the deep earth" or "earth spirits"
Significance: Rooted in the southwest, the Dumnonii's name speaks of ancient connection with the land. They likely practiced deep ancestral veneration and understood the rhythm of the natural world.

7. **Catuvellauni**
Meaning: "Battle chiefs" or "war leaders"
Significance: A tribe of warriors and strategists, the Catuvellauni saw leadership as martial and sacred. Their rulers often led confederations and stood at the edge of British resistance against Rome.

8. **Iceni**
   Meaning: Uncertain; possibly linked to the word for "metal, sword, or iron"
   Significance: The name evokes strength, sharpness, and perhaps transformation. This was the tribe of Queen Boudicca, and their fierce resistance to Roman occupation is legendary. They were likely protectors of both people and spirit.

9. **Trinovantes**
   Meaning: Possibly "the very new people" or "the vigorous ones"
   Significance: Innovators or newly established kin, their name suggests energy, dynamism, and a forward motion. They were allies of the Iceni and part of the old spiritual corridor leading to the Thames.

10. **Silures**
    Meaning: Possibly from a root meaning "seed" or "offspring"
    Significance: This southwestern tribe was known for their fierce independence and wild terrain. Their symbolic role may have involved guarding the genetic and cultural seed-lines of older, deeper traditions.

11. **Brigantes**
    Meaning: Possibly "high ones" or "hill dwellers"
    Significance: Occupying much of what is now northern England, the Brigantes were associated with height — not just geographical, but spiritual. Their name may imply seership, elevation, or guardianship of vision.

12. **Ordovices**
    Meaning: "Hammer fighters" or "those of the hammer"
    Significance: This tribe's identity is clearly martial — the

hammer evokes both war and forging, transformation through force. Sacred blacksmiths, maybe. Their spiritual work may have involved breaking the old to forge the new.

13. Cornovii

Meaning: "People of the horn" (perhaps referring to a geographical shape or totem)
Significance: Whether referencing a horned god, a peninsula, or tribal totem, their name reflects power, virility, and protection.

14. Parisii

Meaning: Possibly "the cauldron people" or "those of the vessel"
Significance: A mysterious tribe from the east, their name could relate to the sacred vessel or the feminine mysteries. Aligned with lunar and ceremonial traditions?

15. Damnonii

Meaning: Uncertain, but possibly related to the Dumnonii — again suggesting deep-earth or sacred-root peoples
Significance: Spiritual cousins of the Dumnonii — wisdom keepers, deep listeners, and walkers of old earth paths.

This chapter serves as a sacred linguistic map — a key to tribal soul. In these names we find the echoes of old gods, the songs of ancestors, and the wind-stirred whispers of totems now half-forgotten. To speak these names aloud is to summon memory, to invoke presence.

In the next chapter, we will explore the symbols, totems, and sacred associations of each tribe, uncovering how animal spirits, natural elements, and sacred geography shaped their identity and role in Albion's great pattern.-

The land remembers. And now, so do we.

CHAPTER 04

BENEATH THE TRIBAL SKY: SACRED SYMBOLS OF ANCIENT BRITANNIA

In the misty groves and broad skies of ancient Britain, every creature, coin, and carved emblem spoke a hidden language of spirit and tribe. The Celtic peoples of Britannia lived by an animistic creed – seeing rivers, beasts, and even the very earth as alive with soul and meaning. To them, nature was not backdrop but kin. A golden eagle wheeling high or a stag in the oak forest might be a messenger between worlds. A tribe's identity was woven from such threads: sacred animals, totemic symbols, and cosmic signs that affirmed their bond with the divine. From the eastern fens to the western hills, each Britonnic tribe nurtured its own sacred imagery. Horses and boars reared in dazzling designs upon their coins – the horse, foremost in frequency, and the boar only a step behind, appearing "prominently in Celtic iconography" and especially on their coinage. These were not mere decorations; they were emblems of power, myths stamped in metal. As we journey through the realms of the Iceni, Durotriges, Trinovantes, Dobunni, and others, we enter a world where symbols were alive with shamanic power. With evocative language preserved in bronze and gold, the tribes expressed sacred kingship, tribal lineage, divine patronage, and the turning of the heavens.

Map of Iron Age Britain highlighting the homelands of key tribes (Iceni in the east, Durotriges in the southwest, Trinovantes north of the Thames, Dobunni in the west, etc.).

ANCIENT BRITICH TRIBES

TRIBAL REGIONS AND SYMBOLS

The Iceni: Horse People of the Sun and Moon

In the far east where the land meets the North Sea, the Iceni tribe rode with the spirit of the Horse. Even their very name may mean "horse people," hinting at a reputation for breeding fine horses and a self-image entwined with that noble creature. Iceni coins recovered from the windswept Norfolk fields reveal a vibrant, unapologetically Celtic style. One common motif shows a powerful boar striding forward, a spear-like line striking through its snout, and above it a solar wheel – a circle with a dot – shining like the sun. On these Iceni "boar" coins, the alignment of spear, boar, and sun forms a shape uncannily like a Chi-Rho cross, centuries before Christ – a cosmic monogram uniting sky and earth. To the Iceni imagination, this design may have carried profound meaning. The boar, courageous and feral, was a guardian of the Otherworld, while the sun-disc oversaw the seasons; together they formed a crossroads between worlds – the earthly and the divine. Scholars note that the cross is a universal symbol of the four seasons and cardinal directions, and its pairing with the boar on Iceni coins likely signified the tribe's cosmic alignment: an acknowledgment that their fate turned with the sun's wheel and the year's cycle. The Iceni warrior-kings, in this interpretation, were sacred guardians of the harmony between sun and soil, light and dark.

Other Iceni coins show galloping horses and crescent moons, reflecting a skyward gaze. Indeed, early British coins in East Anglia often feature twin moons – one waxing, one waning – perhaps symbolising the balance of lunar cycles. In the flat fenlands under a broad sky, the Iceni and their neighbours paid close heed to the moon's rhythms, guiding planting and harvest by its silvery light. The horse on their coinage likely evoked Epona or a local horse goddess – a divine mare who guided and protected the tribe. The Iceni's affinity for horses was so noted that a later Roman writer recorded that the Iceni "were known as skilled horse dealers and breeders". To harness a horse was, for them, to harness a piece of the sun's vitality and the land's fertility.

It is little wonder, then, that the Iceni revered a goddess of victory and sovereignty in the shape of an animal. Their warrior queen *Boudica* (whose name stems from *bouda*, "victory") is said to have released a hare from her cloak before battle, invoking the goddess Andraste to bless their revolt. The hare – a swift creature of the dusk – was sacred; like the chicken and goose, it was considered "contrary to divine law" to eat. The Iceni kept these creatures for augury and companionship, not for the pot, as Caesar observed of Britons' spiritual taboos. To Boudica's host, the darting path of the freed hare was a message from the goddess, a signal that Andraste rode with them. Hare, horse, boar – all were woven into the Iceni's sacred tapestry. In battle, one imagines Iceni warriors wearing boar-crested helmets and torcs of twisted gold, the boar emblems signifying courage and the protection of a war god. Indeed, boar effigies often accompanied Celtic warriors even in death, symbolising ferocity and fertility intertwined. Through these totems, the Iceni proclaimed that their sacred kingship was no mundane authority: their leaders were champions under the sun and moon, riding with the horse-goddess and fighting under the boar's talismanic might. Tribal identity for the Iceni was thus a dance of earthly strength and cosmic sanction – a legacy literally stamped into the coins they left buried in the earth.

The Durotriges: Water's Edge and Earth's Endurance

Far to the southwest, along the chalk hills and rugged coast of Dorset, lived the Durotriges, a seafaring confederacy whose name perhaps meant "dwellers by the water". Isolated by inlets and opposed to Roman rule, the Durotriges developed symbols as stubborn and distinctive as their spirit. Their coinage tells a story of rise and decline: early on, around 50 BC, they struck splendid white-gold staters – likely showing stylized solar horses and whorls – but by the eve of Roman conquest, their coins had devolved into crude bronze casts. As resources waned under economic strain, the Durotrigan artisans simplified and abstracted their motifs. Yet even in abstraction, meaning peeked through. One tiny silver quarter stater bears an image so degenerated that modern eyes discern the outline of a rat upon it. This curious creature, a small snout and hunched back engraved in silver, may have been accidental – the distorted remnant of a once-proud horse motif. But local legend, and some archaeologists, have mused that it was fitting for a tribe possibly dubbed "the water-rat kings". If indeed the Durotriges embraced the rat as a totem of tenacity, it speaks volumes: the rat is clever, resilient, able to survive against odds. Surrounded by marsh and sea mist, beset by powerful neighbours, the tribe perhaps saw in the humble water vole or rat a symbol of endurance and cunning. We can imagine Durotrigan shamans telling tales of a water-holt king, a rodent spirit that outwits larger beasts – a lesson in survival when strength wanes.

The Durotriges did not inscribe the names of kings on their coins ; instead, they clung to the old imagery rich in mystery. The disjointed patterns on their later coins – circles, crescents, and zigzag lines – may have carried on a sacred geometry from earlier times. A fragment of a sun-symbol or a lightning bolt could appear in those abstract designs, hinting at reverence for sky powers even amid impoverishment. Their territory's very soul was water: rivers like the Frome and Stour, and the tides of the Channel. It is likely they honored a water goddess or god of the sea, though the name is lost. Perhaps their warriors painted flowing blue swirls on their bodies, invoking the currents to lend them strength in battle. Roman writers noted that all Britons performed rituals by water and held certain springs and rivers sacred– the Durotriges would have been no exception, especially given their coastal realm. Some of their hillfort strongholds, like Maiden Castle and Hengistbury Head, have yielded special deposits: hoards of slingshots and slain cattle, ritually buried in ditches, as if sacrificed to appease war gods or nature spirits in times of siege. One can picture a Durotrigan druid raising a great bull-horn cup to the stormy sky on the eve of a Roman attack, calling on the bull of the sea or the boar of the forest for protection. (The bull and boar were common sacrificial emblems of strength across Celtic culture.) Indeed, in Celtic myth the boar often symbolizes the potent, untamed forces of nature – forces that the Durotriges, living at nature's edge, surely respected.

For all their fierceness, the Durotriges' spirituality also had a nurturing side. Archaeology reveals they had a tradition of burying grain and provisions in pits, perhaps as offerings to mother Earth for continuing bounty. Among their pottery, certain swirling decorative motifs might represent the waters of life or the coils of a guardian serpent. Such symbols subtly echo the wider Celtic reverence for the Serpent as a keeper of treasures and a protector of waters – even if the Durotriges left no written myth, their art hints at it. In the Durotriges' world, totems were not always bold and golden; sometimes they were small and hidden, like the image of that rat on the coin, quietly asserting that life finds a way. In their refusal to Romanise their currency or culture, the Durotriges expressed a tribal identity rooted in the old magic of the land and sea. Their sacred animals – be it the resourceful rat, the wild boar of the woods, or the timeless salmon of their rivers – spoke to survival, continuity, and the guardianship of home against all odds.

The Trinovantes: Moon Warriors and the Ancestral Bearer of Camulos

In the rich country north of the Thames, the Trinovantes tribe flourished, remembered as one of the first British peoples to make alliance with Rome. Their name has been interpreted as "the very vigorous ones" or "the very new," hinting at youthful energy or renewal. Cantered on the great oppidum of Camulodunum – today's Colchester – they dwelt under the auspices of the war god Camulos, for their capital's name literally meant "fort of Camulos". Camulos, a deity of war and sky, may have been the Trinovantes' patron god, equated by Romans to Mars. It is likely that boar symbols were sacred to him, since on the Continent, altars to Mars Camulus depict a boar as his companion or emblem. We might imagine a Camulos idol in the Trinovantian groves, crowned with antlers or a boar's head, receiving offerings before battle. Indeed, boar crests were common in Celtic military art, and a warrior invoking Camulos would wear the boar as symbol of invincibility and the favour of the Otherworld.

On their coins, the Trinovantes left a legacy of elegant design that married pragmatism with myth. Early Trinovantian coinage (before they were later subsumed by the Catuvellauni dynasty) often shows the crescent moon motif twice over – a waxing and a waning moon side by side. This dual-moon design appears also in neighbouring tribes' coins in eastern Britain, suggesting a shared reverence for lunar cycles in these flatlands where sky signs are prominent. To the Trinovantes, the two moons may have symbolised transition and balance – the eternal return of growth and decline, echoing perhaps the story of a moon goddess who dies and is reborn each month. The presence of this symbol on their currency (the lifeblood of their economy) implies that even in trade and tribute, the tribe acknowledged cosmic rhythms. The people likely held nocturnal festivals under the full moon, and their druids may have timed ceremonies to lunar eclipses or solstices, aligning earthly affairs with the heavens. This is in keeping with Celtic druidic practice, which often calculated time by the moon. A Roman observer might have seen Trinovantian farmers sow by the crescent moon of spring and harvest by the light of the autumn moon, trusting their goddess of the night sky to bless the yield.

Another motif on Trinovantian coins, especially under their later king Addedomaros and then under Cunobelin (who, though of the Catuvellauni, ruled from Camulodunum), was the wheel or solar circle beneath a horse. In one famous type, two crescent moons arc above a prancing horse, and a six-spoked wheel (a sun symbol) adorns the field . This synthesis of sun and moon, horse and wheel, likely carried cosmological meaning – the horse could represent the sun's daily journey or a sky-god's steed, while the wheel spoke to the sun itself or the turning year. It is possible the Trinovantes honored a version of the pan-Celtic sun god *Belenos* or an indigenous solar deity alongside Camulos. If so, the coin's imagery would be a declaration that tribal prosperity comes from the union of sun and moon forces, all harnessed by the tribe's sacred horse.

Trinovantian leaders claimed divine sanction not only through symbols but through mythology. They had a tradition, recorded later by Roman historians, of an ancient lineage: King Mandubracius of the Trinovantes allied with Julius Caesar, avenging his father who was slain by the great chieftain Cassivellaunus. In tribal lore, Mandubracius' family might well have traced their ancestry to a god – perhaps claiming descent from Camulos himself, or from Andraste (the Victory goddess invoked elsewhere in Britain). When Caesar's legions marched into Trinovantian territory, they found a people willing to treat, perhaps because an oracle or druid had discerned that a foreign war god (Mars-Jupiter of the Romans) could be appeased by partnership. We know that the Trinovantes supplied Caesar with provisions in 54 BC and were counted as his allies. Such a pact would be framed in spiritual terms by the druids: the Romans' eagle standard facing the Trinovantes' totemic horse or bull, acknowledging each other's gods. If the tribe kept a sacred animal, it might have been the bull, symbol of strength and wealth, as cattle were extremely important in Celtic society. In Druidic ritual, a white bull was sometimes sacrificed to perceive the will of the gods. Perhaps at Camulodunum's sanctuaries, the Trinovantes performed bull sacrifices to seal the treaty with Rome – the spilling of the bull's blood a pledge between Camulos and Mars.

Ultimately, the Trinovantes' symbols reflect a people who balanced warlike vigour with cosmic attunement. They were, after all, overrun politically by the rising star of the Catuvellauni, yet their legacy lived on in the hybrid culture of Cunobelinus, who ruled both tribes. Cunobelin (celebrated later as "Britain's King of Kings") placed a sheaf of barley on his Trinovantian coins – a bold agrarian symbol of plenty. This ear of grain proclaimed the sacred kingship of prosperity: it linked the king to the fertility of the land, suggesting that under divine favor, Cunobelin's reign brought abundance. Such imagery had mythic resonance – it implied the king as the husband of the Earth Mother, ensuring crops grow tall.

This idea of the king's marriage to the land's spirit is a deep Celtic motif: the sovereignty goddess who confers kingship through sacred union. Though Cunobelin's coin symbols were likely political propaganda, they tapped into this mythic well. The barley ear might subtly echo Rosmerta (a Celtic goddess of prosperity) or the nourishing power of Mother Earth. Combined with the Latin-inscribed name CAMV (Camulodunum) and CVN for Cunobelin, these coins were powerful statements of both worldly authority and divine endorsement. The Trinovantes, through Cunobelin's synthesis, thus projected a vision of cosmic kingship: the king at the center of the wheel of seasons, ordained by the war god and the earth goddess alike. In their tribal identity, we see a melding of myth and realpolitik, all expressed through the timeless language of symbols – moons, wheels, horses, and corn – shining from their treasure and regalia.

The Dobunni: Guardians of the Sacred Tree and Triple Horse

To the west, in the green valleys and Cotswold hills, the Dobunni tribe cultivated a gentler yet no less potent spiritual imagery. Their lands of Gloucestershire and Avon were fertile and rolling, dotted with ancient hillforts like Bagendon and woods that blazed with wildflowers. In Dobunnic lore, one symbol rose above all: the Great Tree. Every gold stater the Dobunni minted (until one ambitious ruler's redesign) bore on its face a striking emblem – a tree-like pattern, branching and spreading. Archaeologists believe this represents the tribal totem tree, perhaps the medlar tree (Mespilus) which gave name to their later capital Corinium. The medlar is a fruit-bearing tree whose Old Welsh name *ceri* is thought to echo in "Corinium," meaning "place of the little pear (medlar)". Whether medlar or oak or apple, the tree on Dobunni coinage was unmistakable. Its stylized form – sometimes looking like a wreath or a flowery pattern – symbolized the World Tree, the axis that connects the heavens, earth, and underworld. In Celtic cosmology, such a tree (akin to the Irish bile or world oak) stood at the center of tribal territory, often literally as a sacred ancient tree where chieftains were inaugurated. The Dobunni's reverence for a tree motif suggests they saw themselves as keepers of the sacred grove, their kings deriving authority from this living symbol of the continuity of life. It is telling that when the Dobunnic king *Bodvoc* decided to assert his personal power, he removed the tree emblem from his coin and boldly stamped his own name instead– an act that one historian likened to replacing a deity's image with a personal advertisement. Bodvoc's move was revolutionary, but even he dared not abandon the tribe's cosmic ties: on his

coins, he added a large sun-ring hovering above his signature three-tailed horse, and within that ring a tiny cross. This sun-cross – a circle with quartering lines – was Bodvoc's nod to the solar deity, acknowledging "the power of the almighty sun-god" extending to all four directions. In effect, Bodvoc said: *I rule, but the Sun rules with me.* The cross-in-ring, an ancient symbol of wholeness and the four seasons, reaffirmed that Dobunnic kingship still bowed to cosmic order.

The three-tailed horse itself was the other hallmark of Dobunnic coin art. On the reverse of many coins, a sleek horse gallops, its tail artfully split into three streaming strands. The Corinium Museum notes that this triple-tailed horse "appears to be the symbol of the Dobunni". We might see this as simply a stylized flourish – yet in a culture where numbers held sacred weight, the triad was deeply meaningful. Three was the number of the goddesses of sovereignty (maiden, mother, crone), of the sacred elements, of the Celtic domains (sky, land, sea). A horse with three tails could denote a beast that runs in all worlds at once, or one guided by a triple deity. Perhaps the Dobunni honored a local horse goddess, akin to Epona, who had a triple form. There is tantalizing evidence of a Dobunnic deity named Cuda or Cudaea – possibly a mother goddess of the locale of Cirencester – whom later Roman inscriptions associate with fertility and plenty. It's conjectured that Cuda was served by cloaked hooded spirits (Genii Cucullati) in local cult, and she might have been symbolized by a great tree or a mare and foal in legend. If Cuda was their patroness, the tree emblem and the thriving horse could both be her insignia: she as the giver of fruit and offspring, of harvest and herds. The mare and tree imagery conjures the idea of the land itself as a fecund mother, one who carries the tribe as a mare carries a foal, and whose roots run deep into the Otherworld.

The Dobunni also drew on broader Celtic myth. Before Bodvoc's assertive coinage, their old gold coins often depicted an abstract sun-god's head – a homage to Apollo-Belenos – with flowing hair that might be mistaken for leaf or flame patterns. This sun-god profile was common in western British tribes, a vestige of Greek influence turned mystic emblem. The Dobunni placed it on one side (obverse) of their staters, while the sacred tree graced the other, signaling a balance of sun and earth: the sky father and the earth mother in unison. When Bodvoc replaced the sun-head with his name, he prudently kept a solar halo above his horse. On one coin, as described, he etched a small cross inside that halo– essentially a solar cross, an image of the Sun whose rays reach the cardinal points. This was more than decoration; it was a spiritual and political message. It implied that Bodvoc had the sanction of the sun god to lead the Dobunni, that he was the sacred king who would maintain the harmony of the four quarters of the land. Removing the ancient tree emblem was a risk, but by venerating the sun in its place, he performed a kind of shamanic bargaining: trading one divine symbol for another, to legitimize his rule.

Interestingly, Bodvoc's very name links to myth – it likely derives from *Boduoca*, related to Bodb, the Celtic war goddess also known as Badb (a harbinger of battle, often manifesting as a crow). Thus, the king who trumpeted his name across the coins also invoked the fierce Crow-goddess in that name. The crow or raven was a powerful totem in Celtic lore, a companion of war deities like the Morrígan, signifying fate and the Otherworld's hand in earthly affairs. We might imagine that Dobunnic war banners or shields bore the painted image of a raven, especially under Bodvoc's reign – a nod to the goddess who granted him "victory" (for *Badb* literally means "crow" and metaphorically "battle-witch"). If the raven flew over Dobunnic armies, it would have been as a guiding totem, a sign that the ancestral war goddess watched over her "victorious ones" (for one theory holds *Dobunni* may come from *bodunni*, "the Victorious"). Shamanic practice might include listening for the croak of ravens or finding omens in the way crows flew before a raid. In more peaceful realms, the butterfly or bee could be minor totems – creatures that flutter among the orchard blossoms of the Cotswolds, seen perhaps as the souls of the departed or messengers of the flower goddess. (Celtic folk belief indeed associated butterflies with the soul and transformation.)

Ultimately, the Dobunni expressed a spirituality that was deeply earth-centred and richly integrative. Their sacred tree connected them to the land's past and future; their triple-tailed horse carried the blessings of sky, land, and underworld in one form. Tribal identity here was tied to being stewards of nature's bounty " –we are the people of the sacred grove, the horse lords of the west" they might have said. Their coins, distributed in two main regional clusters, suggest two subgroups of the tribe, possibly each with its own favored sacred site: one around Bagendon (where coin-minting evidence was found) and another perhaps near Bath or the Severn. Bath's famous hot springs, later dedicated to Sulis Minerva, would in Dobunnic times have been a place of pilgrimage – a portal to the underworld of healing. It is enticing to imagine the Dobunni venerating Sulis (a sun-water goddess) at those springs, alongside Cuda of the medlar-tree. Such overlapping devotions show a people comfortable with a plurality of sacred symbols, each facet reinforcing their connection to the cosmos. Whether under the spreading branches of an ancient tree or beneath the gleam of a noon sun, the Dobunni leadership embodied a shamanic kingship: one hand holding the fruit of the land, the other raising a sun-emblazoned shield, uniting earth and sky.

The Brigantes: The High Ones of the North and Their Goddess

Sprawling across the wild north, from sea to sea, were the Brigantes – by far the largest British tribe in territory, known as the "High Ones". Their name shares its root with Brigantia, the exalted goddess who personified their land and people. In Brigantia, we see the very embodiment of sacred tribal identity: she was at once a mother, a warrior, and a protector. Roman sculptors in later times depicted Brigantia in syncretic form – crowned and winged like Minerva, holding a spear and a globe of victory. On one stone found on Brigantian soil, she bears the Gorgon's head upon her breast, a sign of deadly power, yet holds the globe (the earth, the realm she grants) and a spear (authority and defense). The Roman observer recognised her as Victory itself, Victoria Brigantia, showing that even Rome understood that the

Brigantes' right to rule their rugged hills came from this goddess's favour. To the Brigantes, Brigantia was likely a sovereignty goddess in the purest sense – the spirit of the land made divine, who "confers sovereignty upon a king by marrying or having sex with him" in the Celtic conception. Their Queen Cartimandua, famed in Roman histories, may have been seen by her people as an incarnation or high priestess of Brigantia. It is tempting to think that Cartimandua's marriage to Venutius (and later her taking of a new consort) had religious overtones – a hieros gamos, or sacred marriage, orchestrated to keep Brigantia's favor over the tribe. Indeed, one Greek source hints that a woman named Camma in Gaul took on the mantle of a goddess in such a ritual; by analogy, Cartimandua ("Sleek Pony" in Celtic, another horse reference) might have been ritually wed to the land through Brigantia's rites.

The horse was a recurrent theme for the Brigantes as well. In a hoard at *Stanwick*, believed to be Cartimandua's stronghold, archaeologists discovered a striking bronze horse-head mask. This artefact, beautifully stylised with flowing lines and "lentoid" eyes, likely adorned a ceremonial bucket or cart. Its purpose was more than decorative: it hints that the Brigantes held the horse sacred in their ceremonies, possibly as a totem of sovereignty. In Celtic ritual, the horse was closely linked to kingship – in Irish legend, the inauguration of a king even involved symbolically coupling with a mare and partaking of a broth made from her flesh, a startling metaphor for uniting with the land's fertility. While we have no direct evidence the Brigantes did anything so lurid, the presence of a horse icon in what may have been a royal context at Stanwick suggests that the horse goddess (whether Epona or a local variant) blessed the Brigantian rulers. The horse's head possibly hung at feasts or councils, a silent witness to oaths – a shamanic guardian through which the goddess watched. We can imagine a Druid or bard invoking Epona or Brigantia in the guise of a white mare before the gathered clan chiefs: the chief would place his hand on the bronze horse mask and swear to uphold the land's justice, feeling the cold metal and knowing it stood for the living spirit of the tribe. Archaeological evidence of multiple sets of horse harness in the Stanwick hoard – four sets, in fact, with ornate fittings – reinforces that the Brigantes invested great care and sanctity in their horses and chariots. These were not merely tools of war; they were part of ritual display, possibly used in processions for the goddess at festival times. A Roman writer (Tacitus) later quipped about "the Brigantes under a woman's leadership" nearly defeating Rome– that "woman" could as well be Brigantia personified, riding a chariot pulled by sacred horses into figurative battle.

In Brigantian art – what little we have – we also see the typical Celtic love of swirling patterns and hidden faces. A finely crafted bucket from West Yorkshire depicts running animals and abstract shapes that could be read as both vine scrolls and entwined creatures, hinting at stories now lost. Perhaps these show stags or hounds – other likely totems of the Brigantes. The Brigantian forests were teeming with deer, and the antlered stag often symbolised the forest god (like Cernunnos) or the pursuit of truth in Celtic myth. Meanwhile, a hound was emblematic of loyalty and tracking, and interestingly, one of the Brigantian sub-tribe or family names may have been *Catuvelluni* ("war-hounds") akin to the southern Catuvellauni. The Brigantes, being a confederation, likely had clans each with its emblem – maybe a wolf clan in the Pennines, a stag clan near the forests of Bowland, a boar clan by the eastern wolds. Together under the banner of Brigantia, they unified these animal powers.

Roman era inscriptions give us tantalising hints: one altar calls her Brigantia Caelestis, the Heavenly Brigantia, implying she had a celestial aspect (perhaps a star or constellation was sacred to her – one thinks of the North Star or the constellation of the Great Bear overhead, appropriate for the "High One"). Another inscription refers to Brigantia as a nymph-goddess, highlighting her water aspect; indeed, many springs in the north bore her name, and rivers like the Braint (in Anglesey) recall her. This dual identity – warrior-queen of the sky and life-giving water nymph – encapsulates the Brigantes' world: high crags and flowing rivers, each domain protected by their Lady. It's possible that Brigantian shamans (druids or seers) experienced visions of Brigantia by fasting on hilltops or by descending into sacred wells, seeking her guidance in trance. They may have worn the horned helmet or the bird mask to channel her messages. (Notably, a "Romano-Brigantian theatrical mask" of a human face was found, which might have been used in ritual plays, though that may date to after conquest.)

To speak of Brigantian sacred kingship is to speak of partnership with the goddess. When Cartimandua betrayed Caratacus, handing the anti-Roman hero over to the Romans, some say her favour with Brigantia waned, as her later turmoil with Venutius suggests. Venutius rose as a war leader, perhaps cloaking himself in more traditional piety towards Brigantia (and maybe claiming descent from a god or hero of the tribe). The civil strife could be seen in mythic terms as the goddess testing her people – would they choose the Roman-backed queen or the native warlord? Ultimately, Rome intervened and the Brigantes fell under heavier control. But even then, Brigantia's worship did not die; she was respected and folded into the Roman pantheon as a local aspect of Victoria (Victory). A statue of Brigantia stood at the edge of the empire, spear in hand, reminding Roman soldiers that this land they occupied had its own powerful guardian spirit. The Brigantes thus used their symbols – the crowned goddess, the horse, the spear, the globe of dominion – to assert that their sovereignty came from the divine. In peace and war alike, they remained the tribe of the High Goddess, "Brigantia's children," drawing on her strength as endless as the northern wind.

Threads of Myth Woven in Gold and Stone

Across all these tribes of ancient Britain – whether the horse-riders of the Iceni, the moon-watchers of the Trinovantes, the tree-lovers of the Dobunni, the sea-braving Durotriges, or the proud Brigantes of the north – a common cosmology shone through their diverse symbols. Each tribe had its unique totems and motifs, yet they all shared the fundamental Celtic belief in a universe where the divine saturates every aspect of life. A tribal coin was not a mere currency; it was a talisman, a portable altar in one's pocket bearing the image of a sacred animal or celestial sign. When a warrior grasped a coin depicting a rearing horse beneath a crescent moon, he was tangibly touching the myth of his people – perhaps recalling a tale of how the Moon-goddess once took the form of a white mare to guide the tribe's founders. When a farmer plucked a coin from a hoard showing a corn ear or a tree, he was reminded that the bounty of the land comes from a contract between the tribe and the gods, a contract his king must uphold under pain of famine. The very act of minting these images was likely overseen by druid-wise artisans, who knew that putting an image into the world could invoke the power behind that image. Thus, the process bordered on magic – the hammer striking blank metal, impressing the likeness of horse or boar, sun or moon, in a spark-lit moment that might have been accompanied by a silent prayer.

The sacred animals of Britain's tribes were more than mascots. The horse, the boar, the raven, the stag, the bull, the hare – each carried dense symbolic weight accrued over generations. The boar, for instance, symbolised intransigent courage and often appeared in company with warrior statues, reinforcing that boar's role as an emblem of the warrior's ferocity and fertility. Celtic myth is rife with magical boars – from Torc Triath, the boar of legend owned by a goddess, to the formidable Twrch Trwyth hunted by King Arthur – and these tales were likely told around Britonnic fires as well, grounding tribal boar-symbols in mythic precedent. A young Durotriges fighter hearing of Arthur's boar hunt or the Irish hero Finn's fated encounter with a boar would understand that wearing a boar badge linked him to those epic narratives, granting him a touch of the hero's luck or tragic nobility. Shamanic interpretation was part of everyday life: a druid might guide youths through visionary journeys, urging them to find their spirit animal – perhaps a wolf or a falcon – and to wear its token for personal protection. Totemism, as scholars note, often involved taboos and special reverence. If a clan claimed the salmon as ancestor, they would never harm salmon and would seek wisdom by observing its upstream struggle (salmon being a Celtic symbol of wisdom). If another clan called themselves the Children of the Wolf, they might don wolfskins in ritual dances, invoking the wild hunt in trance.

Crucially, these symbols served to express sacred kingship and cosmic alignment. A Celtic chieftain was not merely a secular ruler; he (or she, as with Boudica or Cartimandua) was the linchpin between tribe and the Otherworld. They were expected to uphold right order (cosmos) in microcosm. The symbols on their regalia – the wheel-pendant on a torc, the solar disk on a shield, the horse standard carried into battle – all proclaimed that the leader had the gods' approval. When these symbols fell – as when Roman eagles eventually cast down the tribal totems – it was seen as the gods' withdrawal from the pact of sovereignty. But during the tribes' independence, the continual renewal of these signs (at winter solstice bonfires, at Beltane feasts, at royal weddings) kept the cosmic harmony. The use of astral motifs like suns, moons, and stars on coins and ornaments suggests the Celts tracked not just seasonal cycles but believed in an intimate linkage: *"As above, so below."* A king might hold a sacred feast at Samhain (summer's end) to mark the death of the year and don a boar mask as he extinguished the hearth fires, only to rekindle them as a sun-wheel come Imbolc (spring's approach), perhaps wearing a golden horse mask to herald the rebirth of light. These rituals would be the living enactment of the myths hinted at by the archaeological finds.

In the soft light of a British dawn, one can almost see it: a circle of druids on a hill, oak leaves in their hair, standing around the chieftain who is seated on a patterned rug woven with spirals and triskele symbols. The chieftain holds a sceptre capped with a bear figurine (for some tribes did honor the bear – the Arth- in Arthur – as a symbol of kingship). The druids chant the lineage of the tribe, invoking Taranis the thunderer, Sucellos the good striker, Epona the mare-mother. As the sky brightens, a ray of sun strikes a bronze shield laid on the ground, whose boss and rims form a solar cross. The head druid lifts a torc – that heavy neck-ring of gold so coveted yet so sacral – and clasps it around the chieftain's neck, declaring him the living representative of the tribe's ancestors and gods. In that moment, all the animals engraved on that torc – wolves chasing their tails, horses entwined with vines – seem to dance in the flickering light. The tribe gathered on the hillside lets out a cry: part exultation, part prayer. They carry banners of their clans: a crimson dragon windsock flutters for one (yes, even dragons, or fiery serpents, had a place in the Briton imagination); a carved boar head on a pole for another; a wooden raven for yet another. The chieftain rises, raises a ceremonial sword to the four quarters, and in each direction the head druid names a guardian: to the east the stallion of dawn, to the south the great serpent of noon, to the west the boar of dusk, to the north the bear of night. The assembled people repeat a solemn vow to keep faith with the land, the sky, and the spirits in between.

Such was the spiritual ethos that the symbols, coins, and totems of Britain's Iron Age tribes expressed. Each coin type unearthed is like a page from a saga: the Norfolk wolf pattern of the Iceni whispering of moonlit hunts and warrior guides; the Cranborne Chase gold of the Durotriges recalling a time of wealth when sun-gold flowed, and its later ugly "potins" telling of hardship but stubborn pride; the vine-leaf coin of King Verica of the Atrebates (a southern tribe under Belgic influence) hinting at Bacchic feasts and the blessings of imported wine , and how even revelry became a sacred act of generosity for a Celtic king. We did not delve deeply into the Atrebates or Cantiaci of Kent, yet they too shared these patterns – King Verica placing that vine leaf on his staters to show both his connectivity to Roman luxuries and perhaps a mystical allegiance to the god of the vine, Liber or a Celtic equivalent. In Kent, early coinage showed wreathed busts and lions under continental influence, but soon turned them into Celtic abstractions: a sure sign that Britannic tribes had their own interpretation of these symbols, likely aligning lions with solar power or kingship, and wreaths with the circle of life.

Through comparative insight, we see the Britons' symbolism was part of a wider Indo-European tapestry: not unlike Vedic kings who underwent ashvamedha (horse sacrifice) to sanctify their rule, or Germanic tribes who took boar and bear as sacred ancestors. The Celts of Britain added their unique accent to this spiritual language. They practiced a distinctly druidic shamanism, one less about solitary shamans and more about a caste of philosopher-priests who guided the collective imagination. Yet, the shamanic element was there: in trance rituals at sacred lakes (where many weapons and ornaments were thrown as offerings), in vision quests at megalithic circles still standing from their predecessors, and in the poetic *awenyddion* (inspired ones) who could channel voices of gods in ecstatic verse. The animals and symbols were bridges to these altered states. A warrior entering frenzy might chant the name of his clan totem " –Grymmaw!" (boar) or "Cŵn!" (hounds) – until he believed the spirit of the boar was running in his veins, making him impervious to pain and fear. A healer might meditate on the pattern of a butterfly's wings or a frog's leap to guide a sick person's soul back from the brink – frogs, after all, were seen as dwellers in two elements (water and land) and thus able to guide between life and death . Every symbol had layers: practical (tribal badge), mystical (connection to a deity or natural force), and cosmological (part of the grand order of the universe).

In this narrative chapter, we have walked the hidden path of the tribes, from the Iceni's sunlit coast to Brigantia's high country. The evocative language of their symbols still surrounds us – on museum shelves and in the ground beneath plow and foot. A Celtic coin's strange, swirly art may look abstract to modern eyes, but it thrums with meaning: a butterfly of the Otherworld here, a solar wheel there, a hidden face of a god in the lines if you look just so. The ancient Britons spoke through those images, and what they say is that *life is sacred, the king is sacred, the land is sacred.* In their world, a king could not be a king without the horse goddess's approval, a tribe could not prosper without honouring the cycles of sun and moon, and no battle could be won without the boar's fearless spirit charging ahead.

The enduring power of these symbols lies in their mythic interpretations. They invite us to see the world as the Celts did: enchanted and interconnected. The tribe and its totem animal were kin; the king and the land were lovers bound by divine law; the turning of the constellations above was mirrored in the patterns woven into a cloak or carved on a shield. This holistic vision, which bridged daily life and eternal cosmos, gave the Britonic tribes resilience and identity amid turmoil. Even as Rome eventually claimed Britain, these symbols did not die – they transformed and slipped into new guises (the boar of the VIIII Legion, the horse of the Saxon White Horse standard, the dragon of the Welsh flag – echoes of the Iron Age still). The legacy of the Iceni, Durotriges, Trinovantes, Dobunni, Brigantes and their kin is thus a rich tapestry of sacred art and story. We have but touched a few shining threads here, but they suffice to show that the hidden path of the tribes was illuminated by the eyes of animals, the light of the sun and moon, and the faith that their ancestors walked beside them in symbol and in spirit. Each coin in the museum, each carved stone or buried offering, is a fragment of that living myth – a call across two thousand years, urging us to listen to the animals, mark the seasons, and remember that we too are part of this great wheel of life that our ancestors so revered.

CHAPTER 05

FOUR SACRED BEINGS: GUARDIANS OF THE ANCIENT BRITISH DIRECTIONS

A Celtic sacred wheel symbolising the four directions and elements. Such motifs echo ancient British cosmology, where each cardinal point is guarded by an animal spirit.

In ancient British spirituality, the world was often envisioned as a sacred circle divided into four quarters, each with its own elemental force and guardian being. Just as the Celts aligned the directions East-Air, South-Fire, West-Water, and North-Earth, our ancestors saw these quarters as alive with spirit. At each cardinal direction stands a Sacred Being – an animal guide who embodies the element of its quarter and watches over the land and its people. These four animal guardians – Adder in the South (Fire), Hawk in the East (Air), Toad in the North (Earth), and Hare in the West (Water) – form a spiritual compass. Together they create a balanced circle of healing and divination, a kind of medicine wheel in the British

Isles that is both unique and yet resonant with patterns found in indigenous traditions worldwide.

Ancient Britons would not have viewed this fourfold arrangement as an abstract system, but as a living cosmology. The fiery summer sun to the south, the sharp east wind at dawn, the misty western dusk, and the cold dark of the north were all animated by these creature-guardians. In ritual and medicine, a druid or wise-woman might call upon the Adder of the South for transformative healing, or the Hare of the

West for guidance in mysteries of the Otherworld. Each creature offered lessons: the snake teaches renewal, the hawk bestows vision, the toad grants stability, and the hare brings intuition. Before exploring each of these beings in depth in later chapters, we first honour them here as a whole – and glimpse how this British wheel of animal powers compares to other peoples' sacred directions, from the tribes of the Americas to the shamans of Siberia and the Celtic kin of continental Europe.

The Adder – Fire Guardian of the South

In the southern quarter, under the noonday sun, coils the Adder, guardian of Fire and summer heat. The adder (the only venomous snake of Britain) has long evoked both fear and reverence. Celtic lore associates serpents with deep wisdom and earth-born magic – the Druids of Wales were even known as *Nadredd*, "serpents," in honour of the adder's mystique. An old Welsh bard famously proclaimed, "I am a wiseman, I am a serpent," equating mystical knowledge with the serpent's power. This fiery creature, gliding over sun-warmed rocks, embodies transformation: it sheds its skin in a cycle of rebirth, just as fire continually renews through consuming the old and sparking the new. In Scottish Highland folklore the adder was a symbol of the Cailleach, the primal Crone goddess of creation, its presence a sign that one stood on sacred ground. Little wonder that encountering an adder on a spiritual journey was said to herald the need to "shed" something in one's life for something greater – the snake's way of teaching release and renewal.

As the Fire Guardian, the Adder was called upon for purification and healing. Ancient healers believed in the adder's medicine: it's shed skin or even its image could ward off illness and evil, much like folk remedies elsewhere used snake charms for protection. Echoes of this persist into the medieval era – for example, the adder stone (*gloine nathair*), a glassy amulet said to be formed from snakes, was treasured by British Druids as a charm of healing and magical sight. In sympathetic folk magic, hanging an adder's slough (skin) in the home was thought to guard against lightning or fire, harnessing the serpent's connection to the fiery forces of nature. The adder's potent venom, paradoxically, could be a cure as well " –like cures like," as medieval physicians believed. We see this in the legend of the toadstone (which often came from an adder's head in lore): it was believed to detect and counteract poison, healing any bite or sting. Such lore shows the overlap of the Adder's elemental Fire with healing – the idea that the same fiery venom which harms can purify and heal when properly wielded.

The symbolism of the serpent in the South has intriguing parallels across the world. Many indigenous traditions also place a great serpent or snake spirit in a position of knowledge and healing. For instance, the shamanic lore of the Peruvian Andes (the Laika tradition) honours Serpent in the South, seeing it as the embodiment of knowledge, sexuality, and the life force of nature. Likewise, some Native American medicine wheels include a snake in their sacred directions – the Hopi, for example, perform an annual Snake Dance to pray for the life-giving rain, recognising the snake as a mediator with the powers of nature. Even in faraway India and Siberia, serpents appear in sacred contexts: Indian Nagas guard treasure and water, and Siberian shamans speak of Ulgermal, a mighty serpent spirit beneath the earth's fire. The ancient Briton's Adder, of course, is a smaller creature than these grand world-serpents, but in the spiritual imagination it was no less potent. As Fire Guardian, the Adder connects Britons to a global archetype of the snake as healer, protector, and transformer – the one who crawls close to Earth's energy yet basks in Sun's flame, uniting earth and fire.

In ritual, facing South to invoke the Adder would fill the circle with a crackling energy. One can imagine a druid tracing the serpent sign in the air and calling: *"Serpent of Fire, wise Adder of the Southern sun, come to us."* This invocation would invite courage, illumination, and the power to transmute sickness or stagnation into vitality. The South, held by the Adder, was therefore the quadrant of passion and rebirth – the spark of life-force that could burn away the unwanted and energise the soul.

The Hawk – Air Guardian of the East

Turning to the East, we greet the Hawk, sharp-eyed herald of the dawn and keeper of the element of Air. At first light, the hawk soars high against the pastel sky, scanning the breath of the land with uncanny vision. In ancient British cosmology, the eastern wind – the *shalest*, the dawn breeze – carried messages from the Otherworld, and the Hawk was its messenger. Celtic oral tradition even lists the Hawk of Achill as one of the oldest animals in existence, a creature of ageless memory and keen sight. Like other birds of prey, the hawk was seen as a go-between linking this world and the spiritual realms. It rides the invisible currents of Air, just as insight and prophecy ride the winds of the mind. The Hawk's virtues are those of Air itself: clear-sightedness, far-memory, and swift inspiration. A medieval Welsh poet might describe a seer as having "a hawk's vision," meaning the ability to see the truth from high above – to discern patterns where others see only confusion.

As the Guardian of Air and the East, the Hawk presides over beginnings and illumination. The East is where the sun rises, bringing a new day; analogously, the Hawk brings new perception and enlightenment. In druidic lore, Air is the element of the mind and spirit, associated with breath, song, and the inspiration of bards. The Hawk's cry at dawn was thus a sacred sound: a call to awaken the soul. To ancient Britons, this bird's appearance could be a sign that the gods were watching or that a message was coming on the wind. We see an echo of this belief in a story from the *Mabinogion* where a hero, upon hearing a bird of prey, gains sudden insight into his quest. Even the way a hawk flew or where it landed might be used for divination – much as Romans practiced augury by observing bird flight, the Celts too could read meaning in the circling of a hawk in the eastern sky.

Across cultures, the East is often associated with a great bird of prey carrying the dawn. Native American traditions in particular revere the Eagle or Hawk of the East: in many Plains and Woodlands tribes, Eagle in the East represents the breath of Spirit, bringing wisdom and vision. The Lakota, for example, honour Wanbli, the eagle, as the East guardian who greets the morning and carries prayers upward on its wings. This is remarkably close to the British idea of the Hawk of the rising sun. In Siberian shamanism, too, the eagle is a paramount spirit – many shamans claim an Eagle ancestor or guide who enables them to fly in the spirit world. One might imagine a Siberian shaman looking to the East and calling upon the Great Eagle much as a druid of Britain would hail the Hawk. The symbols differ only in form, not in essence: both are raptors of the sky, masters of Air, embodiments of foresight and divine communication.

In practice, invoking the Hawk of the East in a ritual would mean invoking clarity and guidance. A healer seeking insight into a patient's illness might face East at dawn, breathing deeply to "take in" the Hawk's vision. A seer or druid might meditate on the hawk feather – considered a precious token – to sharpen inner sight. By aligning with the Hawk, one aligns with Air's qualities: intellect, communication, and the gentle but inexorable force of the wind that carries seeds to new ground. The East is illumination and possibility, and the Hawk, its guardian, opens our inner eyes to possibility.

The Toad – Earth Guardian of the North

In the North, where the land is thick and the nights are long, dwells the Toad, custodian of the Earth element and the mysteries of the winter darkness. At first glance, the common toad may seem an odd sacred guardian – a humble, warty creature that crawls in mud and disappears underground. Yet it is exactly this earthy nature that makes the Toad a fitting Northwatcher. The North in British tradition is the direction of solidity, ancestors, and the deep earth; it is tied to winter and midnight – times when life retreats into the soil to rest. Toads do the same: burrowing into the ground to hibernate through cold months, emerging when the earth reawakens. Thus the Toad embodies Earth's resilience and endurance. It reminds us of the power in stillness, the slow, ancient pulse of the land itself.

Ancient British folklore holds a surprising respect for this little creature. Far from merely a witch's familiar in later superstition, the toad was seen as a healer and a sage of the dirt. British folk medicine included cures like wearing a dried toad to absorb a disease, or using *toad powder* to ward off plagues (albeit these practices emerged more in the post-Roman era, they likely draw on older beliefs about sympathetic magic). The most famous toad-talisman was the Toadstone – a mythical gem said to be found in a toad's skull. This stone, a beloved amulet in medieval times, was believed to detect and neutralise poisons and even ease childbirth. Such virtues align perfectly with the Earth element's domain: protection, sustenance, and fertility. If the Adder's fire could purge illness, the Toad's earth could draw it out and heal it. In a way, the Toad was like a living symbol of the Earth's pharmacy – containing both poison and remedy, embodying the doctrine of "like cures like" as its stone was thought to cure venom.

In the wider context of indigenous cosmologies, a solid, strong creature often holds the North-Earth position – sometimes far larger than a toad. Native American medicine wheels frequently place the great Buffalo or White Bear in the North, representing abundance, grounding, and the endurance to survive harsh winters. The contrast is striking: the Britons chose a small amphibian instead of a hulking mammal. Yet symbolically, the role is similar. The Plains tribes honoured the White Buffalo as the giver of sustenance (food, shelter) in winter, and the Ojibwe and Cree speak of *Makwa* the Bear teaching them to hibernate and heal – lessons of Earth and North. The British toad, too, teaches through hibernation and carries a secret nourishment (for the spirit, not the body). In Siberia, we find another parallel: northern Asian myths tell of a Great Toad or Frog that carries the Earth on its back, or a Cosmic Frog that dives in primordial waters to bring up mud and create land. Siberian shamans commonly have animal helpers like bears and bulls as Earth symbols, but notably they also honour the frog or toad for its shamanic magic of crossing realms. The toad's ability to live both in water and on land – to traverse the marshy liminal spaces – made it a guide between worlds, much as the shaman themselves journey between spiritual and material realms.

For the ancient Britons, the Toad of the North stood at the gateway of winter and the underworld. In ceremonies, facing North and invoking the Toad would ground the circle, drawing protective Earth energy up from the soil. A ritual healer might whisper an incantation to the "Old Toad in the dark earth" asking it to absorb a malady or curse into itself and carry it away into the ground. The Toad's presence was thought to stabilise and sanctify – in practical terms, perhaps a live toad might be kept in a basket during a healing rite, to sympathetically draw out sickness. And in seasonal festivals, the Toad's northward power would be acknowledged at midwinter, when the earth seems dead but is secretly teeming with life waiting to return. The North thus is the quarter of rest, death, and rebirth – the womb of the earth – and the Toad, quietly watching with unblinking wisdom, is its perfect warden. Through the Toad, our ancestors learned the values of patience, persistence, and the hidden fertility within decay.

The Hare – Water Guardian of the West

In the western quarter, where the sun dies into the horizon and twilight veils the world, we meet the Hare – swift-footed guardian of Water and the evening dusk. The Hare has long been a magical creature in British lore, associated with the moon, with goddess energy, and with fortune (both good and ill). To the Celts and Britons, the hare was an uncanny animal: it's nightly dances in the fields and its sudden vanishings into hedgerows made it a creature of transition, just like the liminal West. The West is the direction of the setting sun, of autumn and the gathering darkness, and it governs the element of Water – intuition, emotion, and the boundary between life and death. The Hare fits this realm in symbolic ways. For one, hares are closely linked to the moon and tides; many cultures, including Celtic Britain, saw a hare's form in the patterns on the moon's face. This lunar connection ties the hare to the ebb and flow of water and to the cycle of periodic renewal. Secondly, the hare was sacred to certain British goddesses – most famously to *Andraste*, the war goddess of the Iceni tribe. Queen Boudica, before battling Rome, is said to have released a hare in Andraste's name and interpreted its wild dash as an omen of victory. This act of divination shows the hare's role in prophecy: Britons believed the paths of running hares could reveal hidden truths. The hare's unpredictable zigzag was essentially Water-like – flowing in curved paths, not straight lines – and one had to use intuitive sight to glean meaning from it.

Historical accounts reinforce how revered the Hare was in ancient Britain. The Roman historian Cassius Dio recounts that Boudica's Britons considered it sacrilege to harm a hare, and they would watch intently which way a hare ran as a sign from the gods. Julius Caesar even noted that the Britons raised hares for sacred purposes but forbade eating them. Archaeology backs this, uncovering hare bones buried ritually and bronze hare figurines in Celtic contexts. All this elevates the Hare far above a mere game animal – it was a totem, an oracle, a symbol of the Otherworld. In Celtic myth, creatures that could cross between worlds often appear as hares. There are tales of witches or fairy women transforming into hares to travel at night, evading pursuers until caught by a greyhound (a lore hinting that a hare seen at dusk might be more than it appears). Thus, the Hare carries an aura of shape-shifting and mystery, very much aligned with Water's fluid nature. It represents fertility as well – the famous fertility of hares in spring – connecting the western quarter to life's generative waters and the autumn harvest's abundance (for without spring fertility, there is no autumn harvest).

When comparing the Hare of the West to other cultural symbols, we find both parallels and fascinating divergences. In many Native American traditions, the West is the direction of water, sunset, and introspection, often guarded by a great bear or frog rather than a hare. The bear, like the hare, is linked to the moon (some tribes call the Big Dipper stars a Bear that dances around the North Star, akin to a cosmic hunting story at dusk). The bear's symbolism of going within to heal and reflect parallels the hare's association with intuition and the Otherworld journey. Meanwhile, the idea of a sacred hare/rabbit is not foreign to Indigenous America either – the Algonquian peoples venerate *Michabo*, the Great Hare, a creator hero who is said to have shaped the earth from watery chaos and even to be the offspring of the West Wind. This "Great Rabbit" of the Algonquin is a mighty mythic figure, not a mere animal; yet the choice of hare/rabbit form shares an uncanny resonance with the British hare: both connect to creation, weather, and divine revelation through an animal known for its fertility and elusiveness. In Asian shamanic lore, we also see sacred hares – for instance, in Siberia, shamans' animal helpers include the hare alongside eagles and bears, and in Chinese myth a Moon Hare mixes the elixir of immortality. All these examples underscore an intuitive truth: the hare, worldwide, is often more than a cute or skittish creature; it is a metaphoric well of moonlit wisdom and life's cyclical flow.

In British practice, invoking the Hare of the West would bring the qualities of Water into the sacred circle. A ritual at dusk, for example, might begin by facing West as the sky turns colours, calling on the "Hare of the Hollow Hills" to guide the assembly through the coming darkness. Shamans or druids seeking prophetic dreams would surely ask the Hare's favour – perhaps through a simple divination: releasing a hare (or mimicking one's leap) and reading its course, just as Boudica did. For healing rites, especially those involving emotional or spiritual wounds, the Hare's water element provided soothing, regenerative energy. One could imagine a healer using a cup of spring water (symbol of the West) and invoking the Hare to infuse that water with the power to wash away grief or fear. The hare's connection to the moon also made it a guide for timing rituals – working by the lunar cycles to maximise magical potency, a practice common in Celtic lands. Overall, the West governed by the Hare is the quarter of introspection, endings, and transformation – like the sunset that ends the day or the autumn that ends the growth season, it is both an ending and a gateway to a new beginning. The Hare stands at that gateway, twitching its long ears, ever-ready to leap into the unknown and beckon us to follow.

A Cross-Cultural Tapestry of Directional Guardians

The Four Sacred Beings of ancient Britain – Adder, Hawk, Toad, and Hare – form a pattern that is at once unique and part of a larger tapestry of human spirituality. Nearly every indigenous culture has recognised the sacredness of the cardinal directions, often assigning each a protective spirit or totem animal. This suggests that our ancient Briton ancestors were intuitively aligned with a worldview shared widely across the world:

Native American Parallels: Many Native American nations honour four directional guardians remarkably akin to Britain's. For example, in one common schema the East is guarded by the Eagle (a raptor like the Hawk, bringing vision and messages), the South by the Coyote or Mouse (small, clever animals bringing lessons of adaptation and playfulness, somewhat analogous to the fiery Adder's quick strike and transformative medicine), the West by the Bear (a powerful healer symbolising introspection and the water of life, comparable to the Hare's role in guiding through the otherworldly twilight), and the North by the Buffalo or Moose (great providers symbolising earth, strength, and abundance, paralleling the Toad's grounding and healing aspects). Each tribe's exact animals may differ – the Navajo, Lakota, Cherokee and others have their own sets – but the concept is constant: the four winds each carry spiritual guardians for healing and guidance. The Britons choosing a snake, bird, amphibian, and hare reflects their own environment's fauna, yet the function mirrors the medicine wheel of the Americas: balance in all quarters of life.

• Siberian and Eurasian Parallels: Across the vast steppes and taigas of Siberia, shamanic cultures likewise recognise cardinal spirits. A Buryat or Yakut shaman might not speak of "South" or "West" in the same way, but they do speak of the spirits of the South Wind or the North Mountain. Often these spirits take animal form. We read that Siberian shamans commonly have bears, wolves, and hares as spirit helpers, or majestic birds like eagles and owls for the sky. Among the Yakut people of far Siberia, the North is symbolised by a colossal Bull (Ox) representing the harsh, frigid earth of winter, while the South (associated with the bright heavens) might be watched by the Eagle, and the West by a more ominous figure due to the setting sun's link with evil spirits in their cosmology. The specific associations differ from Britain's – for instance, the Yakut shaman faces East and South for *benevolent* rites, turning North or West only to confront darker forces. But still, the idea of four main directions on Earth each leading to different spiritual realms is pronounced. It's compelling to note that the hare appears even here: Siberian lore counts the hare as a "lesser" helper spirit (for minor shamans) compared to the grand bull or eagle, yet it is present. This mirrors how in Britain the Hare, though physically small, holds a quarter of great spiritual import. Whether on the windswept Mongolian steppe or the Celtic highlands, the cardinal points form a sacred cross, and animals stand at its corners to guide the people.

• Continental Celtic Parallels: The Britons' closest cultural cousins, the Continental Celts (Gauls, Gaels, and their kin in Iron Age Europe), also wove animals deeply into their spiritual worldview. While we have scant direct evidence that Gaulish druids linked specific animals to specific directions, we do know the Celts revered certain key animals across the board: the Boar for its ferocity and courage in battle, the Stag (Deer) for sovereignty and connection to the forest, the Bear for strength (the very name Arthur comes from *Artos*, "Bear"), and the Raven or Crow as messengers of the gods (especially in battle, associated with goddesses like Morrigan). These creatures often appeared on war banners, coins, and sacred artefacts. For instance, Roman reports describe Gallic warriors carrying boar effigies for protection, and archaeologists have unearthed a bronze boar statue at Euffigneix in France thought to represent a local boar-god, perhaps called Moccus. The boar, like Britain's Adder, was associated with both war and prosperity – a paradoxical mix of destruction and fertility. We might imagine a continental Celtic tribe informally aligning the boar with the invigorating South (fire of battle), or the stag with the sunset West (the stag was often linked to the setting sun and autumn rut). Additionally, Celtic mythology frequently invokes *the four directions* in abstract: medieval Irish texts speak of the Four Treasures brought from four cities of the Otherworld, and the early Irish "Settling of the Manor of Tara" describes each cardinal wind bearing unique qualities (knowledge from the east, music from the south, battle from the north, prosperity from the west, for example). While these aren't explicitly tied to animal symbols, they show a shared cosmology where the quartered circle was fundamental. It's very likely that the Druids on the continent had their own correspondences (perhaps taught orally and never written) assigning animal guardians to the quarters during rituals, much as modern Druidic orders do today in revival. The British tradition of Adder, Hawk, Toad, Hare can be seen as one specific lineage of a pan-Celtic (or pan-Indo-European) way of relating to sacred space via animal powers.

In comparing these traditions, what stands out is not the differences, but the underlying unity: a recognition that the *Medicine of the Four Winds* is essential to spiritual balance. Whether it's the Adder or a Serpent, Hawk or Eagle, Toad or Bear, Hare or Buffalo, each culture appointed creatures that resonated with their landscape and soul. The Adder suited Britain's green hills and fiery sun; the Buffalo suited the open plains and needs of Native Americans. The concept of Elemental Guardians of direction, healing, and divination is nearly universal – a testament to how human beings everywhere sought relationship with the living world to find harmony in body and spirit. Each guardian watches not only a compass point but an aspect of life: childhood and dawn (East-Hawk), youth and vigour (South-Adder), maturity and introspection (West-Hare), old age and rest (North-Toad). By learning from all four, a person could live in balance.

Guardians of Ritual, Healing, and Season

For the ancient Britons, these Four Sacred Beings were not distant abstractions – they were woven into daily life, seasonal festivals, and healing rites. Each animal guardian played a role in the ritual year and the medicine practices of the people:

• Ritual and Ceremony: We can imagine a tribal gathering on the eve of a great festival (say Beltane or Samhain) beginning with a calling of the quarters. A circle is drawn, and four callers invoke each animal in turn: *"Great Adder of the South, ignite our circle with your cleansing fire!"*; *"Hawk of the East, lift our prayers on your swift wings!"*; *"Toad of the North, ground us in your enduring strength!"*; *"Hare of the West, guide us through the veils with your intuition!"*. Such an invocation would consecrate the space, essentially asking these guardians to watch over the rite and lend their specific energies. This practice has clear analogues in modern Wiccan and Druid ceremonies (calling the Watchtowers or the four directions), which likely draw inspiration from what Iron Age peoples intuitively did around their sacred groves and stone circles. The presence of these animal spirits would be felt as a balanced wholeness – each quarter of the circle alive and protected, no corner of the human psyche or the natural world left out.

• Shamanic Healing and Divination: In healing, a practitioner might journey in trance to seek one of these animal helpers. For example, if a person was suffering a lingering illness (too much "water" perhaps, in a metaphorical sense of phlegm or emotion), the healer may call in the Adder's fire to burn away infection and rekindle the patient's vitality. They might prepare a poultice heated over coals while singing an adder chant, or literally use an adder-skin in the remedy bag as a talisman of fiery energy. Conversely, if someone was anxious or spiritually "dry," lacking dreams, the healer could invoke the Hare's water to restore emotional flow – perhaps by using water collected under a full moon (the moon-hare's light) and anointing the person, asking the Hare to bring gentle visions. Divination rituals, too, prominently featured these creatures: one seeking guidance might watch the movement of clouds for a Hawk's sign, or cast small bones and look for the shape of a toad or hare in the pattern to interpret the omen. Notably, the historical account of Boudica's hare augury is a prime example of divination with these beings. Even more, the Druids were said to have a practice of *taghairm* (spirit-calling) that could involve animal spirits – one could sit by a waterfall (Water element) until a vision of a hare or other creature appeared with a prophecy. Thus, each of the four beings was a mentor in the unseen, teaching humans how to heal or foretell by attuning to nature's signals.

• Seasonal Rites and Folk Traditions: The cycle of seasons in Britain – spring's rejuvenation, summer's vibrancy, autumn's harvest, winter's withdrawal – was mirrored by the cycle of these four animals. The Hare, for instance, was especially honoured in springtime. Even today, the Easter hare (nowadays bunny) tradition likely echoes an older rite of the spring equinox when hares were seen "boxing" in the fields. This would correspond to the East (dawn of the year) in a ritual sense, even though we've placed the Hare in the West; it reminds us that the animals rotated through seasonal prominence. The Hawk aligns with spring as well, when winds pick up and birds breed – one could imagine a druid at the spring equinox watching the eastern sky for the return of hawks and swallows as a sign of the earth's awakening. The Adder was surely most visible in high summer (South), basking on stones; Midsummer folklore in England holds that on St. John's Day snakes gather in a ball (creating the famed *glibberin* or snake stone). This hint of a summer snake ceremony suggests an ancient acknowledgement of the Adder around the summer solstice, the peak of the sun's fire. Toads and frogs sing loudest at the end of summer into autumn nights, and the toad's appearance in early autumn could augur the coming winter. In some rural parts of Britain, finding a toad in the garden in September was considered good luck for the harvest – perhaps a distant memory of an autumn equinox custom thanking the Toad of the North for the fruits of the earth before hibernation. Finally, in the depth of winter (North), one might think nothing is stirring – but perhaps the shaman, journeying in spirit on a long December night, goes down to the roots of the earth and finds the great Toad sleeping there, and asks it when the spring will come. The turning of the year at Yule might have included rites to honour the Earth Element, the Toad energy, to ensure that the spark of life in the frozen ground would ignite again (sometimes this was symbolised by the log or stone that is heated in the hearth through the night, representing an animal underground – the so-called *nadir* of the sun's journey).

All these imaginings draw from hints in lore and comparative anthropology, painting a picture of how the Four Sacred Animals could have been interwoven with ritual, healing, and seasonal life. What emerges is a vibrant spiritual practice: a cosmology where every direction you faced had a teacher awaiting you. Face the South at noon – find courage and transformation from Adder. Face East at morning – gain clarity and inspiration from Hawk. Face West at dusk – receive guidance through change from Hare. Face North at midnight – draw endurance and wisdom from Toad. In the centre stood the individual (or the community), praying and working within the blessed circle created by these allies.

In tone and practice, this ancient British way has both its own flavour and a kinship with other indigenous ways. It is earthy, poetic, and rooted in the flora and fauna of Britain's soil. It feels "human-sized" – involving creatures that shared the cottages, forests, and fields with the people (snakes under the hedge, toads in the cellar, hawks over the hill, hares in the meadow). There is a natural humility and familiarity in choosing these common yet magical creatures as the cornerstones of cosmology. And yet, it aspires to something universal and transcendent: the great truths of Fire, Air, Earth, Water that all cultures recognise. Ancient Britons found those truths not in distant stars or abstract gods alone, but in the *living beings around them*. In doing so, they created a spiritual language that could be read by anyone sharing the land – farmer, hunter, healer, or child. A language in which a snake crossing your path could be a blessing, a hawk's cry a warning, a toad a comfort, and a hare an invitation to wonder.

Conclusion: Entering the Sacred Circle

This introductory chapter has set the stage by presenting the Four Sacred Beings of the British sacred circle and drawing parallels to other traditions. The Adder, Hawk, Toad, and Hare stand as elemental guardians of South, East, North, and West – each with distinct character and gifts, yet forming one harmonious whole. They guard the four winds, heal the four quarters of the human soul, and open the four gates of perception for the seeker. As we prepare to delve deeper into each of these beings in the chapters to come, we carry forward a few key understandings:

- Ancient British Cosmology: The people of ancient Britain perceived their world as ensouled and interconnected. Their cosmology was not a dry scheme but a lived relationship with certain animals that exemplified the sacred qualities of each direction. This gave them a framework to interpret dreams, omens, and the cycles of nature – a framework grounded in their homeland.

- Elemental Guardians: Each of the four animals embodies its element in both mystical and practical ways. Through the Adder we know Fire's transformative and dangerous power (which can be destructive or healing). Through the Hawk we experience Air's clarity, freedom, and the bridge between worlds. The Toad teaches of Earth's silent endurance and the magic hidden in the lowliest places. The Hare brings the flowing intuition of Water and the wisdom of cycles, change and fate. Together, they ensure that all aspects of life are protected and honored – from the spark of inspiration to the depths of intuition, from physical health to spiritual vision.

- Universality and Uniqueness: By comparing the British Four with those of Native Americans, Siberians, and Continental Celts, we see a universal pattern – humanity's need to partition the compass of life into quarters and appoint *guardians* for each. Yet the specific choice of Adder, Hawk, Toad, Hare is unique to the British context, arising from local fauna and folklore. This reminds us that while spiritual truths may be universal, their expressions are beautifully diverse. The Britons had their own "medicine wheel", as valid as a Sioux medicine wheel or a Taoist four-symbol diagram, speaking in the voice of their land.

- Role in Ritual Life: Finally, we have seen how this fourfold system likely informed rituals of healing, divination, and seasonal celebration. It gave a structure to ceremonies – one that aligns human activity with the cardinal rhythms of the cosmos. When a druid lit a ritual fire, they did so in the presence of the Adder of South; when a seer cast lots, they did so under the flight of the Hawk of East; when families gathered at harvest, they thanked the Hare of West for abundance; when elders told stories in winter, they did so under the blessing of the Toad of North. The Sacred Beings were thus always invoked as partners in the dance of life.

As we turn the page to the next chapter, we will step into the South and meet the Adder in all its depth – exploring how this fiery serpent appears in British myth, what healing secrets it holds, and how one might work with Adder energy today as a source of courage and rebirth. Each subsequent chapter will similarly walk the path of one guardian, allowing us to encounter the Four Sacred Beings not just as abstract symbols, but as living presences we can learn from. By the end of those journeys, we may come full circle, understanding in our hearts what ancient Britons knew: that to walk the "hidden path of the tribes" is to walk always with the guidance of animal kin at the four quarters, in a world where every direction is sacred and every creature carries a spark of the divine.

Calling the Four Sacred Beings: A Rite of Opening

To be spoken with reverence, each facing its direction in turn, beginning in the East.

Face East – The Hawk of Air

Lift your hand or the feather.

"Guardian of the rising light, Hawk of the Eastern skies, You who ride the breath of dawn and see what lies beyond the   *veil, Winged seer, far-eyed prophet, open the gate of spirit and*

speech.
Bring clarity of thought, vision unclouded, the wisdom of the open   sky.
With your cry, awaken this circle. With your wings, stir the soul's knowing."

We welcome you, Hawk of the East, spirit of Air. Come, guide us in truth.

Face South – The Adder of Fire

Light the red candle or hold the ember.

"Guardian of the midday blaze, Adder of the sun-warmed   stone,
Coiled flame, ancient healer, keeper of the sacred spark,
You who shed skin to be born anew, teach us the path of transformation.
Ignite our courage, burn away what no longer serves,
And strike with truth where shadows hide."

We welcome you, Adder of the South, spirit of Fire. Come, guard us in strength.

Face West – The Hare of Water

Touch the bowl of water.

"Watcher of the setting sun, Hare of the western veil,
Moon-dancer, dream-runner, swift one of the hollow hills,
You who leap between the worlds and stir the still waters of the heart,
Carry us into mystery, speak the language of rivers and rain,
And guide our feet through endings toward gentle beginnings."

We welcome you, Hare of the West, spirit of Water.
Come, hold us in grace

Face North – The Toad of Earth

Place your hand on a stone or moss.

"Keeper of the midnight deep, Toad of the sacred soil,
Dweller in root and stone, guardian of all that endures,
You who know the pulse of the buried seed and the silent
drum of the land,
Lend us patience, anchor us in truth,
And teach us how to listen to what grows in the dark."

We welcome you, Toad of the North, spirit of Earth.
Come, bless us with grounding.

Face Centre – The Circle of All

Touch your chest or heart.

"From East to West, from South to North,
By breath, by flame, by stream, by stone,
We open this circle to the old ways.
To the spirits of the land, the memory of the tribes, the song
in the soil,
And to the Four Sacred Beings who stand at the quarters —
Hawk, Adder, Hare, and Toad —
We say:
Come.
Guide us.
Guard us.
And grant us the wisdom of your paths."

Song:"Circle of Four" (Chant for Ritual)

(In a round or solo voice; slow, sacred rhythm with hand drum or a cappella)

Hawk of the East, take flight in my mind

Adder of Fire, leave fear behind

Hare of the waters, run soft through my soul

Toad of the Earth, keep my spirit whole

(repeat 3x, rising in power or fading in to whisper)

CHAPTER 06

THE EAST – VISION AND DIVINE SIGHT

ELEMENT: AIR / DIRECTION: EAST

The eastern wind stirs the soul long before the sun rises. In that breath of pre-dawn, when shadows stretch thin and the birds have not yet cried out, there is a presence—watching, waiting, poised upon the branch of the world. The Hawk, guardian of the East, comes in silence, gliding upon the currents of Air, bearing the gift of sight that pierces illusion. In the cosmology of the ancient Britons, to face the East was to open oneself to the promise of illumination, and to call the Hawk was to seek vision.

The East is the beginning of all cycles, where the sun is reborn and the breath of inspiration first touches the lips. It is the realm of Air—the intangible, invisible force of spirit, speech, and the mind. The Hawk belongs to this realm. Keen-eyed and wide-winged, the Hawk is the messenger of clarity. It flies above the world, untethered, seeing the pattern that hides from those on the ground. When one works with Hawk spirit, one is not merely looking outward, but inward, learning to perceive the deeper truths that rise on the winds of the soul.

Working with Hawk in Divination, Dreams, and Ritual

To call on Hawk is to ask for perspective—to rise above the confusion of daily life and see with the eyes of the divine. In the old ways, omens were often sought at sunrise, when the light was soft and the world most receptive. The flight of a hawk across the eastern sky was seen as a sign, a living line written by the gods. To this day, many who walk the old path will begin their day with a moment of stillness facing the East, whispering a simple invocation:

"Hawk of the Morning Sky, open my inner sight. Show me what I must see."

In divination, Hawk can be invited before any reading—tarot, ogham, or otherwise. Simply placing a feather or token of Hawk (real or symbolic) in the reading space can attune the seeker to higher insight. Some practitioners keep a feather from a buzzard or kite (British birds with strong ties to the raptor lineage) in a sacred bundle, unwrapping it only when insight is truly needed.

Dreamwork, too, belongs to Hawk. To invite the Hawk into one's dreams, one might sleep with a feather or small hawk token under the pillow, or drink a gentle tea of mugwort or vervain before bed while meditating on the image of a soaring hawk. Such dreams may not always be pleasant— Hawk brings truth, not comfort. One may dream of falling, flying, being watched, or of sudden revelations. Keep a journal beside the bed; Hawk teaches in flashes.

In ritual, Hawk is best honored at dawn. A simple practice is to rise before first light, step outside, and breathe deeply while facing East. Speak aloud a truth you are struggling to see clearly. Then remain in silence, listening not just with your ears, but with your whole body. Often, the answer will come not in words but in a shift—a sudden understanding, a lifting of fog. For more elaborate work, create a circle and mark the eastern quarter with feathers, a bird carving, or yellow cloth (Air's color). Light incense that lifts—frankincense, sage, or rosemary—and call:

"Great Hawk of the Dawn Wind, rise within me. Give me the courage to see clearly, and the strength to act upon what is revealed."

Let the incense carry your words skyward. Then sit in quiet. Wait. Hawk always answers, but in its own time.

A Vision Journey with Hawk Spirit

This journey may be undertaken alone or with a guide. Find a quiet place where you can lie down without interruption. Cover your eyes, or let a cloth shade the light. Begin by breathing deeply, steadily, in and out. With each breath, feel yourself lightening, as if the body is becoming less solid, more like wind.

Now imagine yourself standing on a wide hilltop. The sun is not yet risen, but the first light paints the sky in blues and silver. A cool breeze lifts your hair. Before you, perched on a stone, is a Hawk. It watches you with golden eyes. It does not move.

Approach slowly. You need not speak. Simply let your intention rise from within: you seek vision, guidance, truth.

The Hawk spreads its wings. With a beat of air, it launches into the sky—and you follow. Whether your body lifts or your spirit leaves your form, you rise, higher and higher, until the world spreads below you like a great tapestry.

The Hawk flies ahead. Follow.

Let the journey unfold. You may be shown symbols, landscapes, people from your past or future. You may be taken to a mountaintop, a ruined temple, a place from your childhood. Trust the vision. If fear arises, breathe into it. Hawk teaches that clarity often comes after fear is faced.

When the journey begins to fade, the Hawk will return to you. Perhaps it lands nearby. Perhaps it becomes light. Thank the Hawk in whatever way feels true.

Then, breathe yourself back into your body. Wiggle your fingers and toes. Open your eyes. Write down what you saw.

Living with Hawk Medicine

To carry Hawk medicine in daily life is to walk with awareness. It means asking not just "What is happening?" but "What is the pattern beneath it?" When Hawk is with you, synchronicities increase. You may begin to notice signs: a feather in your path, a hawk overhead when you are lost in thought, dreams that do not fade upon waking.

You may also be called to speak truth, even when it cuts. Hawk does not whisper to please. Its cry is sharp, because truth often is. But when tempered with grace, Hawk sight becomes a gift beyond measure—the ability to guide others out of shadow by seeing clearly oneself.

For those who serve as healers, guides, teachers, or artists, Hawk is a powerful ally. It blesses the mind, the voice, and the spirit. Its presence is both sword and song.

In the next chapter, we shall turn from the sky to the coiled warmth of the land—to the South, where the Adder waits among stones, guardian of fire and transformation.

CHAPTER 07

THE ADDER OF THE SOUTH – FIRE AND TRANSFORMATION

Element: Fire / Direction: South

To face the South is to feel the fire of the sun at its highest point, the warmth of summer, and the pulse of life in full bloom. It is the place of courage, growth, and transformation. And at the heart of this direction coils a presence as old as the stones and as fierce as flame: the Adder. The only native venomous snake in Britain, the Adder has long been shrouded in reverence, fear, and myth. Yet to those who walk the old path, the Adder is no enemy. It is a sacred being—a guardian of fire, medicine, and the deep alchemy of change.

The South in many indigenous traditions is associated with Fire, with passion, will, and the trials of becoming. The Adder embodies this. It slides between worlds, close to the earth yet pulsing with inner fire. It sheds its skin in cycles, reminding us that growth demands release. It lies still for hours, conserving strength, and then strikes with precision when the moment is right. In the mythology of the land, it is the awakener, the guardian of hidden wisdom, and the bringer of sacred heat.

The Serpent as a Sacred Being in Britain

Long before the snake was demonised by Christian myth, it was venerated across the British Isles. Ancient Druids were sometimes called "Nadredd" or "serpents," a title of power rather than reproach. The serpent was a teacher of healing and transformation, a symbol of the spiral path of knowledge. Even in folklore, there are traces of this wisdom—the adder stone (a holed stone, sometimes said to form from serpents) was believed to grant second sight and protect from poison. These stones, known in Welsh as *Glein Neidr*, were worn by druids, hung in barns to protect animals, or dropped into wells to purify water.

The image of the coiled serpent appears on torcs, carvings, and amulets throughout ancient Europe. To the Britons, the serpent was not evil but sacred. It was associated with the earth goddess and the underworld, with healing springs, and with the fire of transformation that lives beneath the surface of all things.

Rituals and Spiritual Power of the Adder

The Adder is not a spirit to be approached lightly. It teaches through fire, and fire transforms by burning away the false. To work with the Adder is to invite purification and the forging of a new self. In ritual, the Adder is best called when one stands at a threshold—a moment of great change, a need for courage, or the desire to shed an old identity.

Ritual of the Shed Skin

You will need:

- A quiet outdoor space, ideally in sunlight

- A candle or fire bowl

- A red cloth or stone to represent Fire

- A symbolic item of something you wish to release (a written word, a strand of hair, etc.)

Create a circle. Place the red cloth or stone in the South. Light your candle or fire. Stand facing South and say:

"Adder of the Sacred Flame, coiled one of the sun-warmed earth, I call you now. Come, guardian of

transformation, teacher of fire. Help me to shed what no longer serves, and step into the heat of my true becoming. "

Place your symbolic item into the flame or near it. As it burns or rests, speak aloud what you are releasing. Feel the heat on your skin. Imagine your old self peeling away like skin, and beneath it, something brighter, truer, waiting to emerge. When ready, thank the Adder and close the circle.

This ritual can be adapted for any time of change: solstice rites, the end of a relationship, initiation, or even illness. Fire transforms, but it does so with care when approached in reverence.

Working with Adder in Divination, Dreams, and Personal Practice

In divination, the Adder appears as a sign of change— sometimes sudden, sometimes slow but inevitable. If the image or presence of a snake appears in a reading, dream, or omen, it is often a call to prepare for inner transformation. The Adder teaches us to observe, to wait, and then act with precision. A coiled serpent is not lazy—it is gathering energy.

To work with Adder in daily life, you may:

- Carry a small charm or symbol of the serpent (a spiral, an adder image, or a piece of shed snakeskin if ethically sourced)

- Spend time sunbathing or lying on warm stones, connecting with the heat of the earth

- Practice slow movement meditations that mimic the sinuous grace of the snake

- Reflect on areas of your life where something must be shed for growth

For dreams, the Adder may appear as a guide in subterranean settings, caves, tunnels, or coiled around a source of light. These dreams often mark turning points or initiations. After such dreams, take time to journal, draw the snake, or seek further insight through meditation.

Adder energy is not gentle, but it is wise. It requires respect and self-honesty. Those who resist change may find the Adder's lessons painful. Those who embrace the fire will find clarity, power, and healing on the other side.

A Vision Journey with Adder Spirit

This guided vision should be done when you are ready for deep work.

Find a quiet, warm place. Lie down. Cover your eyes. Breathe slowly and deeply. With each breath, feel yourself relaxing into the earth, as if your body is becoming warm stone.

Now imagine a path of sun-dappled grass. You follow it to a circle of standing stones. In the centre, a coiled Adder lies on a flat rock, it's scales gleaming. You approach slowly, with reverence.

Speak your truth silently or aloud: what you seek to change, what you are ready to release.

The Adder lifts its head. Its eyes meet yours. Without words, it invites you to lie beside it. You do. The warmth of the rock enters your bones. The Adder begins to move around you—not to threaten, but to encircle.

As it coils around you, your skin begins to shimmer. You feel layers falling away. Emotions, identities, old wounds—all peel back. Beneath, something new shines. The Adder hisses softly. Fire flickers at the edge of your vision.

Then, the coils unwind. The Adder slides away, leaving you changed.

Breathe slowly. Return to your body. Wiggle your fingers. When ready, open your eyes and drink water.

Journal what you saw, and what you felt. The Adder teaches through sensation and symbol.

To walk with the Adder is to embrace your power, not with arrogance, but with humility. It is to accept that all things must change—and that within every ending lies a seed of fierce new life. The Adder coils in the South, beneath the heat of the solstice sun, waiting not to strike in fear, but to awaken us to who we truly are.

In the next chapter, we will turn to the North, and the ancient wisdom of the Toad—guardian of the Earth and the depths within.

CHAPTER 08

THE TOAD OF THE NORTH – EARTH AND ANCESTRAL SILENCE

Element: Earth / Direction: North

To face the North is to stand before the oldest gate, the deep root of the world, where time slows and the soul grows quiet. Here, in the thick hush of ancient woods and beneath the dark loam of memory, dwells the Toad—keeper of stillness, guardian of ancestral truth, and sacred companion of the Earth element. There is no glamour in the Toad, no soaring vision or coiling fire. Its power is secret, patient, and profound. To work with the Toad is to enter into the long silence, the deep listening, the inner cave where wisdom sleeps.

The North is the direction of winter, of midnight, of bones and bedrock. It is where the ancestors dwell, where stories linger after voices fade. In the old British lore, the Toad was not simply a creature of superstition but a potent symbol of Earth magic—a being associated with transformation, healing, and protection. It is said that the toad knows the buried pathways, the unseen currents of the land. It carries with it an energy of withdrawal and gestation—teaching us that growth begins in darkness.

The Toad as Keeper of Stillness and Hidden Knowledge

Toads were once considered sacred by many of the old folk. They were thought to guard treasure, both literal and spiritual, and their presence near a home or hearth was a good omen. While later folk belief cast them into the shadow of witchcraft, their earlier symbolism was far richer: they represented the *chthonic* (underworld) aspects of wisdom, the parts of knowing that emerge only in silence, in dreams, or in deep descent.

Unlike the snake, who moves with fire, or the hawk, who rides the wind, the toad stays low. It burrows. It waits. Its movements are slow but purposeful. And yet, within its body lies a strange power—secretion, protection, alchemy. Even its skin, once feared for supposed poison, was used in healing charms and sympathetic magic. The myth of the toadstone, a gem said to grow in the skull of an old toad, speaks to this: a rare treasure gained only by those willing to sit, to wait, to endure.

In this way, the Toad mirrors the Earth itself. It holds, gestates, conceals. Working with Toad is an invitation to connect with the hidden parts of ourselves and the world—to explore the underworld not as a place of fear, but of fertile mystery.

Deep Listening, Shadow Work, and the Underworld

The North teaches us to stop speaking. To listen. In modern life, this is a radical act. But those who work with the Toad know that insight grows in silence. In ritual and practice, the presence of Toad calls for stillness—not the absence of activity, but the deep presence within it. When Toad appears, it is time to go inward.

Practices of Deep Listening:

- Spend time in complete silence each day. Not meditation with a goal, but simply being still and receptive.

- Sit on the earth. Breathe slowly. Ask nothing. Listen to the land with your body.

- Create a "threshold" space in your home or garden—a stone, a bowl of earth, or a hidden corner where you leave offerings to ancestors or spirit. Let this be a place for quiet reflection.

Shadow Work: Toad teaches us that we are not just light. We are compost and decay and unspoken dreams. Shadow work—the practice of exploring the hidden or rejected parts of the self—is sacred under Toad's watch. Begin by journaling without editing. What have you hidden from yourself? What parts of your past still call from beneath the surface?

Work with dark stones (jet, obsidian), with root vegetables, with heavy drums. Go slow. The Toad reveals itself not in haste but in depth.

The Underworld as Womb, Not Tomb: Many fear the word "underworld," imagining only death. But to the ancestors, the underworld was the place of roots, of dreaming, of the ancestors' embrace. Toad guides us here—not to scare us, but to remind us that what is buried is not lost. It is becoming. Like the seed in winter.

piritual Power of the Toad

Ritual of Ancestral Stillness You will need:

- A stone (preferably one found near your home)

- A dark cloth or shawl

- A small bowl of water and salt

At night, or just before dawn, find a quiet place. Wrap yourself in the cloth. Sit upon the earth. Place the stone before you, and the bowl beside it.

Speak:

"Toad of the deep earth, still-hearted one, keeper of silence and shadow, I call you. Teach me to listen. Teach me to wait. Let me hear what lies beneath the noise. Let me remember what I have forgotten."

Dip your fingers in the salted water. Anoint your brow, lips, and chest. Close your eyes. Breathe. Feel the weight of your body. Let yourself drift down—not into sleep, but into slowness. Stay here as long as you need.

When finished, thank the Toad. Pour the water onto the earth. Leave the stone in your sacred space until it no longer calls to you.

Working with Toad in Divination, Dreams, and Ritual

Toad appears in dreams often during times of healing or transition. Unlike Hawk, whose visions are sudden, Toad's insights arrive slowly. You may dream of being underground, in tunnels, or of encountering toads in unusual places. These dreams ask you to look deeper.

To work with Toad energy daily:

- Keep a small toad figure or symbol on your altar

- Use earthy incense (patchouli, vetiver)

- Plant something from seed and observe its cycle

In divination, Toad often appears when we are not yet ready to hear the truth—but need to prepare. If a toad symbol or card arises, take time. Do not rush the message. Sit with it. Write around it. It will unfold.

A Vision Journey with Toad Spirit

Lie on the ground. Close your eyes. Let your breath slow until it is nearly still. Imagine you are standing before a hollow tree at twilight. Its roots open like a door.

You enter.

Down you go, step by step, into the earth. Cool air. Moist soil. At the bottom, a chamber. In the centre, a pool. Beside it sits a great Toad. It does not move. It watches you with golden eyes.

You sit across from it. Silence stretches between you. Then, the Toad begins to hum—a low, deep sound that reverberates in your bones. You listen. Images rise. Memories. Faces. Forgotten dreams. You do not grasp at them. You let them come.

When the sound fades, the Toad blinks slowly. It opens its mouth. From within, it releases something—a small object, a word, a light. This is your gift. Receive it.

Then, rise. Climb back up through the tree roots, carrying your gift.

Return to your body. Open your eyes.

Write or draw what you received.

The Toad of the North teaches us that not all wisdom shines. Some glows faintly in the dark. Some waits patiently in the bones of the land. But all is sacred. All is alive.

In the next chapter, we turn to the West, where the Hare waits at the threshold of dusk—keeper of Water and the mysteries of the heart.

CHAPTER 09

THE HARE OF THE WEST – MOON AND LIMINAL MAGIC

Element: Water / Direction: West

n the twilight hush of the West, where the sun sinks beneath a violet horizon and shadows lengthen into mysteries, the Hare waits. Keeper of moonlight, guardian of liminal spaces, this creature has long danced on the edge of worlds—between day and night, known and unknown. In ancient British tradition, the Hare embodies Water's flowing wisdom, a spirit of intuitive grace, lunar magic, and fertility. Those who journey with the Hare step lightly but deeply, weaving through cycles of transformation and rebirth.

The Hare is a paradoxical guide, at once gentle and fierce, playful yet deeply wise. It is a trickster, evading capture, outwitting hunters, and slipping easily from this world to the Otherworld and back again. Linked intimately with lunar goddesses, fertility rites, and the sacred feminine, the Hare represents not only physical fecundity but also creative and spiritual renewal.

Lunar Goddesses, Shapeshifting, and Fertility

The moon has always whispered through Hare magic, connecting it deeply with goddesses who govern tides, cycles, and intuition. Celtic goddess Eostre—associated with spring and renewal—famously claimed the Hare as her sacred animal. Similarly, the Hare was connected to Andraste, the fierce warrior goddess invoked by Queen Boudicca. In folklore, hares were seen as magical shapeshifters, embodying human spirits or deities, running free under the lunar glow.

Their swift and elusive nature made them symbols of fertility and rebirth. The Hare's prolific breeding mirrored the abundant energy of the earth awakening in spring, linking it to renewal rituals and celebrations. To encounter a Hare was considered a potent omen, a sign of forthcoming abundance or an impending shift in fortune. Its liminal nature—occupying both land and spirit realms—made it a powerful ally for those seeking guidance in transitions and transformations.

Boudicca's Hare Ritual Revisited

The historical account of Boudicca releasing a hare before battle reveals deep roots in ancient divination. It was said she observed the path the Hare took—forward or back, left or right—to determine the outcome. This wasn't mere superstition; it was a deeply spiritual act of reading the patterns of nature.

- Modern practitioners can adapt this practice symbolically:

- On the night of a full moon, create a sacred space outdoors.

- Hold a stone or carved figure representing a hare. Clearly voice a question or intention regarding an important decision or transformation.

- Place your symbol gently on the ground and watch for subtle signs—the wind's direction, the rustle of leaves, or the movement of nearby animals. Let the natural world offer its guidance.

The power of Boudicca's ritual lies in surrendering to intuition and trusting the symbols nature provides

Working with Hare in Divination, Dreams, and Rituals

Hare's presence in divination often signals a time of heightened intuition and emotional fluidity. Dreams of hares frequently bring messages of impending transformation, fertility (creative or literal), and spiritual awakening. To work effectively with Hare in daily practice:

- **Moon Connection:** Align rituals with lunar phases, especially the full moon (manifestation) and new moon (renewal).

- **Dreamwork:** Place hare imagery or figurines near your bed to invite potent dreams. Keep a dream journal close by to record and reflect upon any insights.

- **Intuitive Ritual:** At twilight, take a bowl of clear water outside, reflecting the moonlight on its surface. Speak your intention into the water, asking Hare to guide your intuition. Leave it overnight, then use this water for blessings or to anoint objects for intuitive work.

A Vision Journey with Hare Spirit

Find a peaceful place were you feel safe and relaxed. Lie comfortably, close your eyes, and allow your breathing to become gentle and slow. Imagine standing at the edge of a misty meadow as dusk descends. Moonlight begins to spill across the land.

In the silver glow, a hare emerges, ears alert, eyes bright. It pauses, watching you carefully. You silently convey your wish—to journey, to learn, to transform.

The Hare bounds forward; you follow with effortless ease. It leads you swiftly through landscapes that shift—fields, forests, and shimmering streams, all bathed in moonlight. Feel yourself becoming lighter, more intuitive, your senses finely tuned.

Eventually, the Hare brings you to a liminal place, perhaps a quiet grove or sacred stone circle bathed in lunar radiance. It stops, turning toward you, its eyes reflecting ancient wisdom. Without words, it imparts a message—a symbol, an image, a feeling—that resonates deeply within your heart.

Thank the Hare for its guidance. Return slowly to your body, carrying the Hare's gift of insight. Ground yourself gently, moving your fingers and toes, breathing deeply. Open your eyes, and take time to journal or sketch your experiences.

Living with Hare's Wisdom

In daily life, Hare energy invites you to trust intuition and emotional wisdom. Practice heightened awareness, noticing synchronicities and signs. Keep your movements fluid, adaptable. Trust your instincts, and when uncertainty arises, reflect quietly by moonlight or near water.

Hare reminds us that transformation is a continual dance of endings and beginnings. Embrace the shifting nature of life's tides, and like the Hare, learn to navigate both the seen and unseen realms gracefully.

As we conclude this chapter, we step from the lunar glow back into our waking world, carrying the Hare's gentle, potent magic. In the chapters ahead, we will weave together all we have learned from the guardians of Air, Fire, Earth, and Water, exploring how these four sacred beings form a timeless compass for spiritual wisdom and growth.

PART III

COSMOLOGY AND PRACTICE

CHAPTER 10

THE FOUR DIRECTIONS AND THE CIRCLE OF TOTEMS

In the spiritual traditions of ancient Britain, the world was not seen as linear, but cyclical—a great wheel that turned through the seasons, guided by the wisdom of animal spirits and the cardinal directions. Each direction—East, South, West, and North—holds its own sacred guardian: Hawk, Adder, Hare, and Toad. Together, they create a balanced circle of elemental energy, guiding us through ritual, divination, and personal transformation.

Building a Brittonic Wheel of the Year

The Brittonic wheel of the year is a sacred framework aligning personal practice with the natural rhythms of the land. To construct this wheel, we combine seasonal cycles with the four sacred animal spirits. This wheel helps anchor spiritual work in nature's cycles, deepening awareness and connection to the environment.

- **East (Spring Equinox):** The Hawk, guardian of Air, marks new beginnings and inspiration. At this time, rituals can focus on planting intentions, fresh starts, and intellectual orspiritualgrowth.

- **South (Summer Solstice):** The Adder, guardian of Fire, embodies energy, passion, and transformation. Rituals here involve celebrating achievements, vitality, and invoking courage for personal challenges.

- **West (Autumn Equinox):** The Hare, guardian of Water, presides over intuition, reflection, and emotional clarity. Rituals focus on gratitude, letting go, and understanding emotional truths.

- **North (Winter Solstice):** The Toad, guardian of Earth, represents stillness, introspection, and ancestral wisdom. This season is ideal for rituals of deep meditation, shadow work, and honouring ancestors.

As the year turns, marking these significant points helps practitioners attune to nature's deeper rhythms, reinforcing the cycles within their own lives.

Using the Four Animal Spirits in Ritual and Divination

Incorporating the four animal spirits in your rituals enhances your connection to each element's energy, deepening your intuitive skills and spiritual practice.

- **Hawk (East):** Invoke Hawk during divination for clarity and vision. Place feathers or air symbols on your altar, burn incense, or stand facing east at dawn to call Hawk's guidance. Hawk supports clarity, new ideas, and truthful communication.

- **Adder (South):** When you seek transformation or courage, invoke Adder. Use candles, red stones, or symbolic serpentine imagery to invite its fiery energy. Adder guides you through significant changes, encouraging bravery and renewal.

- **Hare (West):** Invoke Hare during intuitive rituals or when seeking emotional healing. Water offerings, moonstones, or reflective surfaces like bowls of moonlit water enhance its presence. Hare helps you navigate emotional complexity, offering intuitive insights and graceful transitions.

- **Toad (North):** For rituals involving grounding, ancestral work, or shadow exploration, invoke Toad. Use earth symbols, dark stones, or bowls of salt and soil. Toad guides you through deep listening and inner journeys, anchoring you to ancient wisdom and patience.

In divination, symbols representing these animal spirits—cards, stones, or carvings—can clarify situations or guide decision-making. Draw a token or meditate with each spirit to reveal hidden truths and pathways.

Creating Your Own Totemic Altar

A totemic altar dedicated to the four directions and their animal spirits provides a tangible anchor for spiritual practices. It serves as a sacred space to honour cycles, perform rituals, or seek guidance.

Steps to build your altar:

1. **Select Your Space:** Choose a quiet, respectful corner of your home, garden, or natural setting.

2. **Align with Directions:** Clearly mark each direction. East faces sunrise, South the midday sun, West sunset, and North towards midnight or polar stars.

3. **Represent Animal Spirits:** Place a symbolic representation at each directional point:

- East (Hawk): Feathers, incense, air symbols.

- South (Adder): Candles, fiery crystals, serpent imagery.

- West (Hare): Water bowls, moonstones, reflective items.

- North (Toad): Stones, earth, ancestral objects or heirlooms.

- **Centre the Wheel:** At the centre, place a sacred object symbolising unity or wholeness—a stone, bowl, or symbolic wheel.

- **Using your altar:**

- **Daily Connection:** Each morning or evening, face each direction briefly, acknowledging its guardian and asking for guidance.

- **Seasonal Celebrations:** Perform rituals on equinoxes and solstices, decorating the altar seasonally and honouring each spirit in turn.

- **Personal Rituals:** Bring specific concerns or intentions to the altar, lighting candles, making offerings, or simply meditating.

Practical Ritual Example:

A simple ritual could be:

- Face East: "Hawk, grant me vision and clarity."

- Face South: "Adder, lend me courage and strength."

- Face West: "Hare, guide me gently through change."

- Face North: "Toad, anchor me deeply in wisdom."

Conclude by touching your central object: "In balance and gratitude, I walk the sacred circle."

Living the Sacred Circle

Working consistently with the Four Directions and their animal spirits is transformative. Over time, you will notice enhanced intuition, emotional balance, spiritual insight, and a profound sense of connectedness. The sacred circle is not merely a ritual space but a living framework that shapes everyday life, infusing ordinary moments with meaning and harmony.

This path is gentle yet powerful, rooted in nature and nourished by ancient wisdom. Through regular practice and sincere connection, you embody the sacred wheel, discovering profound truths in the simplest gestures of daily life. The animal spirits guide, support, and inspire you, reminding you always: life is cyclical, wisdom is elemental, and your journey is never taken alone.

CHAPTER 11

DIVINATION OF THE TRIBES

In ancient Britain, divination was more than mere fortune-telling—it was an intimate conversation between humans, the land, and the spiritual realms. Tribal communities relied heavily on interpreting signs from nature, movements of animals, and omens hidden in everyday occurrences. By reviving and reconstructing these traditional techniques, modern seekers can access profound wisdom, strengthen intuition, and deepen their connection to ancestral ways.

Reconstructed Techniques: Omens, Animal Signs, and Movement

Ancient Britons placed significant importance on observing the natural world, believing it continuously communicated messages from the spiritual realm. Omens and signs were read in animal behaviours, weather patterns, and even subtle shifts in the environment.

- **Animal Omens:** Animals served as messengers. Observing their behaviours provided clues about the future or insights into current challenges. The sudden appearance of certain animals, such as hares, hawks, or snakes, carried specific symbolic meanings:

- **Hare:** Symbolised intuition, fertility, and imminent change.

- **Hawk:** Represented clear vision, messages from the divine, and impending truth.

- **Adder:** Signified transformation, hidden danger, or powerful shifts about to unfold.

- **Toad:** Indicated grounding, ancestral presence, and the need for introspection.

- **Movement Patterns:** Tribal seers watched carefully for subtle signals, such as the direction a bird took flight, the way a hare crossed their path, or the pattern of an adder's movement across the land. Each direction had meanings:

- **East:** New beginnings, inspiration, clear thought.

- **South:** Strength, transformation, active energy.

- **West:** Emotional depth, intuition, transitions.

- **North:** Stability, introspection, ancestral wisdom.

To practice, spend quiet moments outdoors, noticing what creatures appear and how they move. Record these encounters in a journal and reflect on the patterns that emerge over time.

Creating and Reading Signs Using Sacred Tools

Divination in the Brittonic tradition often employed sacred tools—natural items charged with spiritual intent—to read signs and gain insights.

- **Sacred Stones (Lithomancy):** Stones collected from sacred sites or rivers were tossed onto the earth or a cloth. Their positions, shapes, and arrangements revealed symbolic meanings:

- Circular patterns represented cycles or wholeness.

- Linear alignments suggested clear paths or direct actions.

- Clustered stones indicated complexities or interwoven issues.

- **Animal Tokens**: Small carved animal figures or symbolic objects representing the four sacred totems (Hawk, Adder, Hare, Toad) were used similarly:

- Place them randomly and interpret their positions relative to one another.

- Meditate upon each token, drawing intuitive impressions that connect to current life circumstances.

- **Natural Elements**: Leaves, feathers, and twigs collected with intention can be scattered upon a marked circle or altar space. The patterns formed offer messages:

- Feathers represent thoughts or communication.

- Leaves symbolise growth, decay, and transformation.

- Twigs indicate paths, crossroads, or decisions to be made.

- Regular practice strengthens intuitive abilities, making your interpretations more precise and personally meaningful.

The Dream of the Hare, The Shadow of the Adder

Dream divination held immense significance among ancient tribes, offering profound insights and guidance from the subconscious and spiritual realms.

- **The Dream of the Hare**: Dreams involving hares often signify a time of intuition, emotional revelation, or impending transition. The Hare's elusive nature symbolises hidden truths coming to light. To engage more deeply:

- Keep a dream journal to record hare dreams immediately upon waking.

- Reflect on emotional states and personal situations that correspond with hare appearances.

- Use hare imagery near your sleeping space to encourage dream visitations.

- **The Shadow of the Adder**: Dreams of adders can represent fear, hidden threats, or powerful transformation. The shadow of the adder urges you to confront deeper fears or suppressed truths:

- If an adder appears, note its behaviour—coiled, moving, striking—each carries a different meaning.

- Meditate upon the image to understand what personal transformation or healing is required.

- Perform rituals of release or empowerment following such dreams, utilising adder symbolism (candles, shedding imagery, fiery stones).

Practical Divination Ritual

A simple divination ritual to integrate these techniques into daily life:

- Choose a quiet, natural setting. Gather sacred tools—stones, animal tokens, feathers.

- Clearly state your question or intention.

- Scatter your items gently onto a cloth or sacred circle.

- Observe the positions and relationships between objects.

- Note initial intuitive reactions before applying symbolic meanings.

- Record your insights and reflect upon them over time.

Through dedicated practice and respectful engagement, these ancient methods provide clarity, deepen spiritual connections, and offer reliable guidance. The wisdom of the tribes remains alive, accessible, and profoundly relevant, illuminating paths forward and honouring the deep heritage of Brittonic spirituality.

CHAPTER 12

RITUALS OF THE OLD WAYS

The Old Ways of ancient Britain thrived through daily rhythms, seasonal celebrations, and sacred rites honouring the land, ancestors, and spiritual realms. Rituals were woven deeply into everyday life, marking the turning of seasons, acknowledging nature's cycles, and maintaining a harmonious balance between humans, spirits, and the Earth. Today, by reconnecting to these practices, we reclaim a vibrant spiritual heritage, enhancing our personal growth and nurturing our bonds with nature and ancestry.

Daily, Seasonal, and Sacred Rites

Rituals anchor our spiritual practices, allowing us to consciously interact with the natural world and spiritual forces. Daily, seasonal, and sacred rites create rhythm and structure, guiding us through the cycles of life:

Daily Rites:

- **Morning Salutation**: Upon waking, greet the sun and thank the East for inspiration and clarity. Acknowledge the animal spirit of the Hawk for clear vision throughout your   day.

- **Evening Reflection**: At dusk, give gratitude to the West for emotional wisdom and intuitive insights gained. Acknowledge the Hare, reflecting on the day's emotional and spiritual lessons.

Seasonal Rites:

- **Spring Equinox (East)**: Celebrate new beginnings with planting rituals, lighting candles, and placing flowers or feathers on your altar to invoke Hawk's clarity and fresh vision.
  Summer Solstice (South): Honour personal growth and transformation. Create a fire or light candles, invoking Adder's strength for courage and decisive action in your life.
  Autumn Equinox (West): Offer gratitude for abundance. Hold water-based rituals, intuitive meditations, and reflective journaling, guided by Hare's emotional insight.
  Winter Solstice (North): Engage in introspection, honouring ancestors and ancestral wisdom. Perform shadow work, meditation, and grounding rituals

involving earth elements, guided by Toad's stability and ancient knowledge.

Sacred Rites:

- **Initiation Rituals**: Mark personal transformations and life transitions—births, coming of age, marriage, elderhood—with rituals invoking the four sacred animal guardians and elemental energies for guidance and support.

Honouring Land Spirits and Tribal Ancestors

Connecting with land spirits and ancestors strengthens your roots and deepens spiritual awareness:

Land Spirits:

- Create a dedicated outdoor space for offerings—stones, herbs, water, or natural items.

- Regularly visit this sacred place, leaving respectful offerings, acknowledging the spirits of trees, rivers, and stones.

- Spend quiet moments meditating or simply listening to the land, acknowledging its presence and guidance.

Tribal Ancestors:

- Establish an ancestral altar in your home, placing heirlooms, ancestral images, candles, and meaningful objects.

- Regularly leave offerings like water, bread, salt, or favorite foods of your ancestors.

- Speak to your ancestors regularly, seeking their wisdom and sharing your life, reinforcing your bond with the lineage of wisdom and experience that supports you.

Songs, Chants, and Offerings

- Songs and chants have long been powerful mediums for communicating reverence, intent, and connection during rituals. Offerings represent tangible gestures of gratitude and respect:

Songs and Chants:

- Use simple, repetitive chants during rituals to align energies and focus intentions:

- East: "Hawk on the wing, clarity you bring."

- South: "Adder fire bright, courage in the night."

- West: "Hare soft and wise, truth before my eyes."

- North: "Toad deep and strong, roots where I belong."

  ○ Sing traditional or personally meaningful songs during seasonal celebrations to elevate collective energy and communal bonds.

Offerings:

- Offerings are gestures of reciprocal respect and gratitude:

- **Water**: Represents emotional clarity and intuition, ideal for honouring the West.

- **Fire**: Candles or small fires symbolise transformation and strength, fitting for the South.

- **Earth Items**: Stones, soil, or plant materials anchor energy, suitable for the North.

- **Incense and Feathers**: Represent air, clarity, and communication, perfect for the East.

- Each offering reinforces mutual respect and strengthens your relationship with spiritual entities, ancestors, and natural elements.

Practical Example Ritual

- A simple, powerful ritual to honor daily or seasonal cycles:

- Clearly mark a circle outdoors or indoors, aligning with cardinal directions.

- Begin facing East, acknowledging Hawk: "Spirit of air, inspire me."

- Move clockwise to the South, invoking Adder: "Spirit of fire, transform me."

- Continue to West, honouring Hare: "Spirit of water, guide my heart."

- Finally, turn North, grounding with Toad: "Spirit of earth, anchor my soul."

- Place an offering at the circle's centre, thanking the spirits and ancestors for their presence.

Practicing these rituals regularly fosters profound connections, enriching your spiritual life with wisdom, gratitude, and reverence. The Old Ways provide timeless guidance, keeping ancient traditions vibrantly alive within our hearts and lives.

PART IV

ECHOES IN THE LAND
CHAPTER

CHAPTER 13

HOMELAND OF THE DUROTRIGES AND THE EARTHBOUND KINGS: DORSET'S ANCIENT TRIBE AND A FAMILY'S LEGACY

Map: A parchment-style map showing the ancient British tribes and their territories, with the Durotriges domain in

southwestern Britain (modern Dorset and environs).

In the rolling green downs of Dorset – amid chalk hills, fertile valleys, and Iron Age earthworks – echoes the ancestral presence of an Iron Age people called the Durotriges. For the modern family tracing its roots in places like West Compton and Cann, this land is more than a picturesque corner of England: it is my *ancestral homeland*, rich with the memory of an ancient tribe. The story of the Durotriges in and around these Dorset villages is a story of continuity and connection. It weaves from the Iron Age, when tribal boundaries first crisscrossed these hills, through medieval records of land and lineage, and into the present moment as descendants seek to reconnect with the spirit of their forebears. This chapter explores that journey – blending historical richness with a humanised, poetic touch – so that anyone yearning to rediscover their own tribal and land-based roots might find both inspiration and guidance here.

Ancient Dorset: Land of the Durotriges

More than two thousand years ago, the region now known as Dorset was the heartland of the Durotriges tribe. The Durotriges (possibly meaning "fort dwellers" in Brittonic Celtic tongue) were one of the Celtic tribes of Britain living here prior to the Roman invasion. Their territory spanned much of modern Dorset, spilling into parts of today's Wiltshire and Somerset, and extending westward until meeting the lands of the Dumnonii tribe near the River Axe. To the east, their domain reached toward the River Avon, abutting the lands of the Belgae. In essence, all of the Dorset countryside – from its chalk ridges to its coastal cliffs – was Durotrigian land. West Compton and Cann, nestled in North Dorset's valleys under what is now Shaftesbury, lie well within this ancient Celtic realm. We can imagine that the ancestors of those villages walked under the same Dorset sky in Durotrigian times, knowing the same rolling hills and winding streams, and calling this place home.

The culture of the Durotriges was deeply intertwined with this landscape. They were agrarian people, raising crops and livestock on the fertile soils of the Dorset vales, yet ever mindful of defence – hence the nickname "fort dwellers." Across their homeland, they built impressive *hill forts*: great ringed ramparts of earth crowning the hills, which served as communal strongholds and symbols of tribal identity. Some of Britain's most famous Iron Age hill forts rise in Durotriges country, their grassy ramparts still visible today. Maiden Castle near Dorchester, for instance, is among the largest hill forts in Europe, and according to legend was fiercely defended by the tribe when the Romans arrived. In the north, nearer to West Compton and Cann, the tribe's footprint remains in the mighty earthworks of Hambledon Hill and Hod Hill, which loom above the Blackmore Vale. Archaeologists tell us Hambledon Hill was developed into a *major Iron Age fort by around 700 BC* – a strategic citadel guarding trade routes along the River Stour. Just across the valley, on Hod Hill, the Durotriges erected wooden palisades atop earlier earth mounds, a testament to their determination to protect their land. Indeed, when the Roman army under Vespasian swept through Dorset in AD 43, they found these hill forts as formidable obstacles. On Hod Hill the invaders even resorted to siege engines, bombarding the ramparts with iron bolts from ballistae as they fought to dislodge the tribe. Although the Durotriges ultimately succumbed to Roman conquest, their connection to the land remained unbroken – the blood of the tribe flowed on in the local population, and many hill forts were not entirely abandoned but repurposed or quietly revered.

The Durotriges' way of life blended practicality with a spiritual connection to place. They buried their dead in crouched positions in oval graves, often with personal goods for the afterlife. Women in Durotrigian society appear to have held remarkably high status; recent archaeological studies of graves and even DNA analyses suggest a *matrilocal* pattern, where households were organised around maternal kin lines. We might imagine Durotrigian mothers and grandmothers passing down stories of the land to their children – stories of sacred springs, ancestral mounds, and the spirits of those who came before. Their settlements were clusters of roundhouses with thatched roofs, likely surrounded by small fields and grazing lands bounded by the dense oak forests that once covered much of Dorset. In places like present-day West Compton, it's easy to picture a Durotrigian farming hamlet: cattle lowing in the pastures at dusk, smoke curling from hearth fires, and beyond the hedgerows the silhouette of Hambledon Hill standing guard. The tribe struck their own coins (bearing stylised horses and pagan deities) and traded along the coast – evidence of a vibrant local economy and culture rooted firmly in Dorset soil.

By the time Rome's influence took hold, the Durotriges had begun to adapt. The Romans established a town at Durnovaria (modern Dorchester), essentially co-opting the Durotriges' main settlement as a regional capital. Over the next few decades, the tribe's identity merged into a Romano-British one. Villas appeared in the countryside, Roman roads cut across old tribal boundaries, and Latin words mingled with the old Celtic tongue. Yet, notably, the land itself still nurtured the descendants of the tribe. In North Dorset, many native families continued to farm their ancestral plots through the Roman era and into the chaotic early medieval period that followed Rome's retreat. When the Saxons eventually pushed into Dorset (around the 7th century), the "land of the Durotriges" was absorbed into the rising kingdom of Wessex. Even so, the people living here – the early inhabitants of villages like Compton and Cann – were likely a blend of newcomers and the old Durotrigian stock. The tribe's *fate was sealed* in political terms, but their legacy lived on at the grassroots: in the continued occupation of the land by their progeny, in local folklore, and in the very bones of the Dorset earth. Every generation, whether they knew it or not, was building on the foundations the Durotriges had laid.

Medieval Roots: From Tribal Lands to Family Lands in West Compton and Cann

As centuries passed and Britain's tribes faded into history, the once-tribal lands of Dorset became the patchwork of medieval manors and parishes we recognise from records. By the Middle Ages (12th–16th centuries), West Compton and Cann were small rural communities under the feudal system – a world of lords, manors, and yeoman farmers. Yet, these places remained, in essence, the same cherished *homeland*, now tended by the descendants of those who had always been here. To walk through West Compton in, say, the fifteenth century would be to find a cluster of farmsteads in a sheltered valley (the Saxon name *Cumb-Tun* literally meant "valley farmstead"). The Abbey of Shaftesbury, a powerful Benedictine nunnery founded in the 10th century, held sway over this area. In fact, West Compton was recorded as Cumpton Abbatisse " –the Abbess's Compton" – reflecting that it belonged to the Shaftesbury nuns since at least King Edwy's grant of 955 AD. The Domesday Book of 1086 confirms this continuity: it lists *Compton Abbas* (encompassing what we now call West Compton and East Compton) with a sizeable community of 32 households, all under the lordship of Shaftesbury Abbey. Nearby villages like Melbury Abbas and Fontmell were similarly listed as Abbey possessions. These records show that, a thousand years after the Durotriges, the land was still in essentially communal stewardship – now in the hands of a religious institution, but worked by local families who had likely tilled the soil for generations.

One of those local families in later medieval Dorset carried a surname that echoes down to the present: Hascoll (also spelled Haskell, Hascall, and other variants). It is in the

1400s–1500s that we first catch glimpses of this family name in the records of West Compton and surrounding parishes. Genealogical research suggests that a certain Thomas Huckyll (an early spelling of Hascoll/Haskell) was born around 1455 in West Compton. This Thomas is believed to have died by 1496, but already was established family in the area. His son, recorded as Robert Huckehull (Haskell), was born circa 1480 in the nearby village of Fontmell Magna and later lived in West Compton, dying there in 1557 according to compiled pedigrees. These tantalising fragments indicate that the Hascoll/Haskell clan were freehold farmers or copyholders in this patch of Dorset from the late medieval period. As tenants of the Abbey's manor (and later of secular lords after the Dissolution), they would have farmed the same fields that lay under the shadow of ancient hill forts, perhaps very aware that their very presence represented a line of continuity from tribal times. It is poetic to imagine that when Thomas Hascoll plowed his strip of land in 1500, turning up dark Dorset earth and flint nodules, he might even have unearthed an old sherd of Iron Age pottery – a silent testament to his deep-rooted heritage in that soil.

The name Hascoll itself hints at local origins. According to one account, *Haskell/Hascoll* likely means "the marsh dweller" – perhaps derived from Old English or Welsh, describing someone living by wetlands. In North Dorset, the valleys (like the Blackmore Vale below Compton) were once marshy in parts, so it's plausible the family name sprang from the landscape itself. What's clear is that the Hascoll/Haskell surname is strongly associated with Dorset and neighbouring Wiltshire, appearing in no great frequency outside this region. This suggests the family was not Norman nobility but indigenous folk, rooted to the area from olden times. By the early 17th century, we find the spelling "Hascoll" explicitly in records – for example, a 1613 mention of a Thomas Hascoll in the village of Cann, Dorset. Cann is only a few miles from West Compton; it sits on the slopes just south of Shaftesbury, with green pastures and hedgerows stretching toward Fontmell. The appearance of the family name there and in Fontmell Magna in the 1500s and 1600s indicates that the family's branches spread gently through the adjoining parishes, maintaining a tight geographic circle. They were certainly yeoman farmers – the sturdy middle-class of old rural England – neither lofty barons nor landless peasants, but customary landholders who often passed their farmsteads from father to son for generations. In an era when landownership defined one's security, the Hascolls seem to have managed to hold onto pieces of their ancestral turf.

Landownership records from the 1400s–1500s in Dorset further illuminate this picture. While detailed deeds from that period can be scarce, a variety of documents give us snapshots of who held land in West Compton and Cann. For instance, medieval manorial court rolls for the Manor of Compton (if we could read them) would list tenants' names, fines, and transfers of copyhold land. It is very likely that the Hascolls appear in such rolls as copyhold tenants of Compton Abbas manor or as jurors in the manor court, given their long residence. We know that after 1539, when King Henry VIII dissolved the monasteries, Shaftesbury Abbey's vast Dorset estates (including West Compton) were confiscated by the Crown. In 1540, the manor of Compton was granted to Sir Thomas Wriothesley (Earl of Southampton), and shortly after sold to Sir Thomas Arundel. The Arundel family would have then been the new lords of the manor, but they, like the Abbey before them, depended on the local families to actually work the land. Thus, the 16th-century Hascolls likely transitioned from being tenants of an abbess to tenants of a nobleman, with their obligations and rents now owed to a secular lord instead of a convent. Surviving records such as tax rolls of the Tudor period provide further evidence: the Lay Subsidy rolls of 1524–1525 (a tax assessment) for Dorset often list the names of householders in each tithing. It would not be surprising if a "Haskoll" or "Huckoll" appears paying tax in the Compton or Cann area, indicating a person of some means (since the very poor weren't taxed). By the Elizabethan era, the family was well established; one Thomas Haskell (perhaps spelled "Hascall") born around 1539 in Cann lived until 1613, leaving behind children who would disperse further or even emigrate (indeed, Haskell descendants were among early New England colonists a few generations later, carrying Dorset memories across the Atlantic). Through all these records, a remarkable thought emerges: *the Hascolls held on to their little portion of the old tribal land.* In feudal documents they might be "tenants" rather than free tribal proprietors, yet in a deeper sense they remained keepers of the ancestral ground, generation after generation, as the world around them changed.

Before moving on, pause to consider the image of those medieval and Tudor-era ancestors in West Compton and Cann. In the fifteenth century, they might have gathered under the ancient yew tree in the churchyard of East Compton's medieval church (whose crumbling 15th-century tower still stands today). Perhaps they heard stories of the giants of the old hills – folk memories of the Durotriges turned into legend. By the seventeenth century, a Hascoll child in Cann would have looked out from the family cottage and seen the great ridge of Melbury Beacon rising nearby, unaware that on that very hilltop, ages past, a beacon fire may have been lit as a warning when Roman legions approached. The continuity of family and land is almost tactile here: the Hascolls ploughed fields that had been cleared by Celtic farmers, they raised sheep on pastures where prehistoric barrows lay hidden, and they drew water from springs that had quenched the thirst of

Romanised Britons, Saxon shepherds, and everyone since. This unbroken presence, from tribe to medieval tenant to modern descendant, imbues the Dorset landscape with a profound sense of belonging.

Tracing Lineage Through Time: Tools for Unearthing Ancestral Landholders

How can one today uncover such deep roots? The journey of connecting a present-day family to an ancient tribal homeland is a detective adventure through historical records and genealogical resources. In the case of the Dorset families like the Hascolls, a variety of tools and documents have helped illuminate the path. Anyone seeking to rediscover their own lineage in a particular place can learn from this process. Below, we explore the key resources and how they shed light on the chain of ancestry from the Durotriges era onward:

• **Domesday Book (1086):** This great Norman survey is often the earliest detailed record for any English locale. In our story, Domesday provides a baseline for West Compton (Compton Abbas) shortly after the Norman Conquest. It notes, for example, that *Compton Abbas had 32 households and was held by Shaftesbury Abbey* as lord in 1086. While Domesday does not list common folk by name, it names the lords and gives a sense of the community size and resources (plough lands, mills, livestock) at that time. For a researcher, Domesday confirms which estates existed and who controlled them. In Dorset's case, knowing that Shaftesbury Abbey owned West Compton and nearby manors tells us where later monastic records might be found. It also shows continuity – the fact that Compton was populous in 1086 suggests a thriving village likely descended from late Saxon (and

Brittonic) inhabitants. Thus, Domesday ties the ancient tribal land to the medieval administration: what was once Durotrigian territory became a named manor recorded by Norman scribes. Modern tools like the Open Domesday database allow researchers to easily find these entries and understand their context.

• **Manorial Rolls and Estate Records:** After Domesday, for the next several centuries the primary records of land occupancy are manorial documents. Each manor (such as the Manor of Compton Abbas, or the Manor of Cann if it was distinct) held regular court sessions where tenants' dealings were recorded. The Manorial Court Rolls and Rent Rolls can be a goldmine of ancestral information. They often contain the names of tenants, transfers of land (for example, when a tenant died and his heir took over, or when a copyhold was sold), local disputes, and even inventories of fields. In Dorset, thousands of these records survive – many preserved at the Dorset History Centre in Dorchester. The Dorset History Centre has collections from estate archives (like those of the Rolle family, Pitt-Rivers family, etc.) which include manorial rolls for parishes across the county. For instance, a diligent researcher could consult the Manorial Documents Register (MDR) via the National Archives to find what records exist for Compton Abbas or Cann. These might include 16th-century court rolls noting that "John Haskoll paid a heriot of one ox upon the death of his father to inherit a tenement at West Compton" – an entry that would tangibly link the family name to that land in that era. Our narrative used secondary sources that summarised such findings (like genealogical compilations), but seeing the original manorial entry in Latin would be a thrilling confirmation. It's worth noting that manorial records can date back to the 1200s in some cases. They bridge the gap between Domesday and parish registers. While they require some effort to access and translate (often written in abbreviated Latin), they are vital for tracing landholding families in the 14th, 15th, and 16th centuries. In our case study, we suspect the Hascoll/Haskell family appears in these rolls by various spellings – these records would show their status (copyhold tenant, perhaps owing a few days' labor to the lord or an annual rent in shillings). The fact that by the 1500s the family was still there is indirectly evidenced by these sources. For a broader audience, the lesson is: *to trace your lineage into medieval times, look for manorial documents for the estates where your ancestors lived.* They can confirm family presence and even relationships long before church records began.

• **Parish Registers (16th century onward):** With the introduction of parish registers in 1538 (under Henry VIII's minister Thomas Cromwell), a new window into family history opened. Parish registers are the records kept by the parish church of baptisms (christenings), marriages, and burials. In Dorset, many parishes have registers surviving from the 1500s or 1600s. (For example, Compton Abbas's registers start around 1640, while some nearby parishes begin a bit earlier.) These registers allowed us to follow the Hascoll/Haskell family tree generation by generation. A baptism entry might read, say, "1570 – Joane, daughter of William Haskoll of West Cumpton, baptised the 3rd of May," and a burial entry decades later could record "Buried – William Haskoll, an old man of Cann, September 1613" (which aligns with the known death of Thomas/William Hascoll). By compiling such entries, one can reconstruct family units and migrations between parishes. Early parish records can be patchy – the English Civil War, for instance, caused some gaps (we noted Compton's registers pause in the 1640s during the turmoil). However, they remain the backbone of genealogical research from the Tudor era onward. Modern researchers benefit from many Dorset registers being transcribed or indexed online (via resources like the Dorset OPC – Online Parish Clerk – project, or commercial databases). In our narrative journey, parish registers confirmed that the Hascoll family stayed rooted in the region through the 17th century, with branches appearing in records of Fontmell Magna, Cann, and neighboring hamlets. If you too are tracing ancestors, diving into these yellowed pages (often available on microfilm or as digital scans) is like time-travel: you see your forebears' names recorded by a long-dead vicar's quill, solidifying their existence in a specific *place and time.*

  • **Land Records and Maps (18th–19th centuries):** To connect the more distant past to the edge of living memory, tithe records and early maps are extremely useful. The Tithe Commutation Act of the 1830s produced detailed tithe maps and apportionment books for each parish, which list every plot of land, its owner, and its occupier (tenant) at that time. For example, the tithe map of West Compton (Compton Abbas West) in 1842 exists, and its accompanying schedule from 1843 names who owned each field and who farmed it. If the Hascoll family still held property then, they would appear as owners or leaseholders on that list. Even if they had moved on, the tithe survey provides a snapshot of the village that can be compared with earlier eras. Additionally, enclosure awards and estate maps from the eighteenth century (if any were made for the area) might show ancestral lands. In our case, by the 19th century, surnames may have shifted due to marriages and economic changes, but tools like the census records (from

1841 onward) can take over, showing Haskell descendants as farmers, labourers, or emigrants. Yet, for linking to the tribal past, the tithe map is especially symbolic: it's essentially a map of who held the land, not so different from a Domesday Book for the 19th century. Using it in tandem with older records, one can sometimes trace the occupancy of a particular farm or plot back through various documents across centuries. Many a genealogist has stood on a piece of ground with these old maps in hand, realising "this wheat field numbered 112 on the tithe map was the very acreage my ancestor leased, and perhaps it fed our family line for generations."

• **Other Resources:** There are, of course, many other records that fill in the tapestry. Wills and probate records can be illuminating – a will from 1600 of a Dorset yeoman might mention "my tenement in West Compton to my eldest son" and name all children (precious data for lineage tracing). Tax rolls (like the Subsidy rolls and Hearth Tax of later 1600s) list names and can confirm an ancestor's economic status and location. The Domesday Book, manorial rolls, parish registers, and tithe records we highlighted are some of the main pillars for deep historical research, but combining them with wills, census, gravestone inscriptions, old newspapers, and local histories truly brings an ancestral story to life. In our Dorset case study, we have not only identified names and dates for the Hascoll family, but also connected them to specific plots of land, to wider historical events (like the Dissolution of the Monasteries), and even to the ancient context of the Durotriges. Anyone embarking on a similar quest should cast a wide net: check if local archives have a manorial court roll index, search for your surnames in published county history books, look at archeological surveys of the area (perhaps your ancestor's cottage sits atop Roman foundations!), and even

DNA test to see if genetic signals echo an ancient continuity in the region. Each tool is like a candle shining into the past, and together they can illuminate the path where family lineage meets tribal legacy.

Reclaiming the Ancestral Connection Today

Standing on a Dorset hilltop at dusk – say, atop Hambledon Hill's windswept ramparts or by the weathered stones of an old Compton farmstead – one can almost *feel* the presence

An artistic illustration of a Celtic knot in fiery red, symbolising the enduring spiritual bond between descendants and their ancestral lands.

of those who came before. For descendants of families like the Hascolls, whose lineage threads back into the

mists of the tribal era, the connection to the land is not only historical but spiritual. To walk the footpaths of West Compton and Cann today is to walk in the footsteps of one's ancestors, stretching back generation upon generation, perhaps as far as the Iron Age. In an age where much of life is transient and globalised, this realisation – that *"my blood and*

my surname are rooted in this very soil" – is profoundly grounding. How might one symbolically or spiritually reclaim a sense of tribal land rights or ancestral presence in Britain today, especially when the literal ownership of the land may long ago have passed out of family hands? The answer may lie in acts of remembrance, stewardship, and immersive reconnection with the ancestral landscape.

First, there is knowledge and acknowledgment. Simply learning about the Durotriges and knowing *"this was their land and thus my land"* is an act of reclaiming heritage. When a descendant acknowledges the ancient name of the land (for example, calling Dorset "the land of the Durotriges" in thought or speech), they pay homage to the first known stewards of their home. One might engage in personal or family ceremonies of acknowledgment: visiting local Iron Age sites like Maiden Castle, Badbury Rings, or Hambledon Hill and quietly honouring those ancestors. A visit to Maiden Castle's summit at sunrise, for instance, can be a spiritual pilgrimage – envisioning tribal sentinels on the ramparts and perhaps leaving an offering of wildflowers or a libation to the earth, in the manner our distant ancestors might have honoured the land spirits. On a smaller scale, tending the graves of known forebears in the local churchyard or placing a memorial plaque for the family on ancestral property (if accessible) can be deeply meaningful. Though the legal title of the fields of West Compton may belong to someone else in the modern day, nothing prevents the descendants from *reclaiming those fields in their heart.* Walking the perimeter of an ancestral plot, one can speak the names of the known ancestors who lived there, essentially staking a spiritual claim: "Here my people dwelt; their essence remains and I, their child, return."

There is also the aspect of cultural revival and continuity. To reconnect with tribal roots, many people explore the traditions and spirituality of those times. For Britons of Celtic ancestry, that might mean studying Celtic folklore, learning a few words of the old Brythonic language (Cornish or Welsh, cousins of the Durotriges' tongue), or even participating in modern druidic or pagan practices that draw from Celtic myth. One might celebrate the seasonal festivals once observed by the ancient Celts – such as Imbolc, Beltane, Lughnasadh, and Samhain – as a way of syncing one's life to the agricultural and cosmic rhythms that guided the Durotriges. Imagine gathering with family on a high hill on Midsummer's eve to light a bonfire, knowing that two thousand years ago your ancestors might have done the very same to mark the solstice. Such symbolic acts create an emotional bridge across time. They allow descendants to inherit the role of custodians of tradition and environment, even if in a symbolic way. Some have even crafted family crests or emblems incorporating ancient tribal symbols (for example, a Celtic knot or a stylized hillfort image) to signify the fusion of old and new identities. The illustration above of a radiant Celtic knot is one such symbol – it speaks to the eternal interweaving of lineage, land, and legacy, the fiery red evoking passion and life-force linking generations.

Importantly, reclaiming ancestral presence is not about legal possession or exclusivity; rather, it's about renewing a relationship. In Britain today, all lands have passed through many hands – from tribes to kings, from abbeys to gentry, from gentry to modern homeowners or the National Trust. A descendant of the Durotriges cannot roll back history to tribal ownership, but they *can* assert a form of spiritual ownership: a sense of belonging so profound that the land and the person feel as one. This can be fostered through acts of care. For instance, volunteering for local conservation projects (hedge restoration, forest planting, or footpath maintenance) in one's ancestral area is a way of giving back to the land. It echoes the ancient responsibility the tribe would have felt – to nurture the earth that in turn nurtured them. If one's family historically farmed a certain hillside, perhaps one can symbolically "re-farm" it by planting a small heritage orchard or even just a single tree there (with the current owner's permission), creating living continuity. In our Dorset narrative, a Hascoll descendant might arrange to plant an oak on the old homestead in West Compton, commemorating the family's 500+ year presence. That oak, taking root in the chalky soil, would stand as a guardian linking past and future, a witness that *the line is unbroken.*

For those unable to physically engage with the land (due to distance or access issues), storytelling and writing become powerful tools of reclamation. This very chapter is an example: by writing the family's story intertwined with the tribal history, the descendant-author is actively reclaiming their heritage. The written word immortalises the connection, ensuring it isn't lost to time or memory. One might compose a poem or song about the ancestral homeland – perhaps singing of "Compton in the Combe and the tribe of old" – as a form of personal anthem. Sharing these stories with the next generation is equally vital. When a parent takes their children to the ruins of Shaftesbury Abbey and says, "Here our fore-mothers and fore-fathers prayed and worked, and on these hills before that, our tribal ancestors stood watch for Roman armies," they pass on more than facts; they pass on identity. The child, absorbing this, grows up with an innate sense that they too are part of this land's saga, entrusted with its ongoing story.

Finally, there is a subtle yet profound reclamation that happens within the mind and soul of the seeker. As one delves into genealogy and local history, one often feels the veil between present and past grow thin. In walking the ancient paths, you might catch yourself feeling that you *remember* something you've never been told – a deja vu, a resonance deep in the bones. Many who pursue ancestral reconnection report a sense of guidance or companionship, as if the ancestors walk with them. Standing in the medieval church of Compton Abbas, quiet and sunlit through stained glass, a descendant might close their eyes and feel gratitude welling up: gratitude to the named and unnamed forebears who kept the flame alive through dark ages and hard times so that *you* could be here now. In that moment of gratitude, one is indeed communing with the tribal soul. You realise that you are the living continuation of all these lives – a representative of the Durotriges in the 21st century, one might say. With that realisation comes a sense of *homecoming*. No matter where you go in the world, a part of you will always hark back to Dorset, to those green hills and chalk valleys. And should you ever feel lost or uprooted, you know you can return to that homeland – even if just in spirit – and draw strength from it.

In Britain today, there is a growing appreciation for indigenous heritage (even as Britons ourselves are indigenous to these isles in a historical sense). People are beginning to speak of the ancient Britons with the same respect usually given to more distant indigenous cultures. By symbolically reclaiming tribal land rights, descendants assert that the connection between a people and their land is sacred and enduring. It's a gentle assertion – one that doesn't seek to undo the modern world, but to infuse it with ancient wisdom. For the Durotriges' descendants, that wisdom might be: *Honour the land as your ancestor. Remember that your identity is woven from this earth. Protect the hills and rivers, for they in turn protect your story.* In practical terms, this could mean engaging in local heritage projects, supporting the preservation of Iron Age sites, or even campaigning for the environment of Dorset (for example, opposing developments that might destroy archaeological layers or natural beauty). Each such action is a step toward fulfilling a kind of tribal stewardship in a modern context.

As a case study and guide, the tale of the Hascoll family in Durotrigian Dorset teaches us that finding one's tribal and land-based roots is a journey of both intellect and heart. It requires research – poring over old records and maps – and it requires openness to ancestral memory – listening to the land and one's own heritage with humility and reverence. In reuniting with our tribal homelands, we do not become stuck in the past; rather, we become whole in the present. We stand, as the proverb goes, on the shoulders of giants (quite literally on the giant earthworks of hillforts!), seeing farther and understanding ourselves better. The ancestral homeland of West Compton, Cann, and greater Dorset now lives in the Hascoll descendant's imagination not as an abstract place but as an extension of family. The hills are kin. The old Durotriges capital of Dorchester becomes an ancestral city, and the Celtic tribeswoman buried with her mirror in a Dorset barrow may well be claimed as great-grandmother a hundred times removed. By embracing this continuity, we carry forward the treasures of the past – identity, belonging, wisdom – into the future.

In conclusion, to anyone seeking their own "hidden path of the tribes": let this Dorset journey serve as an example. Research diligently, for the records of your ancestors await in dusty tomes and digital databases. Walk the land they walked, feel the same wind that kissed their faces. Celebrate and preserve the culture and nature of your homeland, because through you, your tribe still lives. And remember that reclaiming your heritage is not about possessing land or glory, but about rekindling a sacred relationship. The ancestral spirits – whether called Durotriges or by any other name – surely smile when we, the living, remember them. In the end, *we* are the land and the land is us, an inheritance indivisible. The tribe is not gone; it sleeps in our genes and our collective memory, waiting for us to awaken to its presence. In West Compton and Cann, that awakening has begun – a homecoming of the heart to the tribe of the chalk hills and green coombes, to the Durotriges, our ancient family. Welcome home.

CHAPTER 14

BOUDICCA'S DREAM AND THE MOON'S RISING

Boudicca's Dream: In the dark hush before the revolt, Queen Boudicca of the Iceni is said to have dreamed of a moonlit goddess rising over Britannia. In her vision, the full moon – pregnant with light – climbed blood-red through tattered clouds. A hare darted in the silvered grass at her feet, and an owl cried from an ancient oak. Boudicca beheld a tall woman in white, face painted with woad spirals, standing beneath the lunar disc. This phantom queen's eyes blazed like embers. In a voice both tender and terrible, she whispered of vengeance and freedom. Awaking in a cold sweat, Boudicca understood: Andraste – the tribal war-goddess – had spoken. The Romans' time was ending; the tribes' ancient mother was rising. She carried this dream like a torch in her heart as she summoned her people.

The Queen's Vision Under the Moon:

By the next full moon, Boudicca gathered the chiefs of the Iceni and neighbouring tribes in a sacred grove. The council of British leaders met in a ring of oak and yew, their faces lit by flickering torches. Boudicca stood before them tall and unbowed – a warrior queen with long tawny hair falling to her hips, clad in a cloak of plaid and a great golden torque at her neck. At her side stood her two young daughters, bearing witness to their mother's resolve. They all knew the Romans had dealt her unspeakable wrongs: her husband's kingdom annexed, Boudicca herself flogged, and her daughters raped, in a brutal attempt to break the spirit of the Iceni. But instead the Romans had awoken something fierce and holy. As the chiefs murmured and the night air hung heavy with anticipation, Boudicca raised her spear. Under the moon's gaze she recounted omens that had appeared across the land – the Romans' own statues toppled and rivers run red – as if the goddess herself foretold a great uprising. The assembled Britons shivered; some swore they could feel the earth tremble with the ancestors' approval.

Then, with the dignity of a high priestess and the ferocity of a general, Boudicca delivered her rallying cry. History remembers her speech not just as a political appeal, but as a sacred incantation before battle. In the silence of that council, broken only by the crackle of firelight and the sigh of wind through leaves, her voice rang out:

"You have learned by actual experience how different freedom is from slavery... Now, let us do our duty while we still remember what freedom is, that we may leave to our children not only its name but its reality. For if we utterly forget the happy state in which we were born and bred, what, pray, will they do, reared in bondage?"

Warriors who had grown up under the yoke of Rome felt their hearts surge at her words. Freedom – the very thing their fathers and mothers had cherished – was now theirs to reclaim. Boudicca evoked the old ways, the "ancestral mode of life" the Romans had tried to erase. She reminded them that although Rome had brought trinkets and taxes, they had taken everything that mattered: land, wealth, dignity, and even the sanctity of family. The queen's voice was clear and human, resonant with sorrow and steely hope. She spoke of how much better it was to live poor and free than rich and enslaved, and how even death was preferable to life under Rome's unending demands. Heads nodded around the circle of chiefs; many had themselves paid cruel taxes and seen their loved ones abused.

Boudicca's tribal identity shone through each line. She addressed not just the Iceni, but all Britons as kin – *"my countrymen and friends and kinsmen... seeing that you inhabit a single island and are called by one common name"*. In a land often divided by clan rivalries, she invoked a deeper unity: the Britons as one people under the protection of the goddess of the land. This was more than a strategy; it was spiritual kinship. By calling them children of the same mother (the land itself), she bound their fates together. She urged them to remember the happy freedom of their ancestors and to fight so that their children would inherit that freedom in reality, not just in memory. In this way, her speech became almost prophetic – a charge to fulfil the destiny laid by past generations. Many listeners felt as if their forefathers' spirits stood behind them in the shadows, nodding in agreement.

Boudicca did not shy away from pointing blame at the Romans, yet she also turned the responsibility back onto the Britons themselves. *"It is we who allowed them to set foot on the island in the first place,"* she admitted ruefully. By acknowledging this, she transformed guilt into determination: they *must* correct that ancient mistake now. The chiefs thumped spears against shields in approval, eyes shining with tears of rage and hope.

She then spoke of the enemy with cutting scorn and insight. The Romans, she said, might have armour, walls, and discipline, but they lacked the Britons' bravery and hardiness. She painted a vivid contrast: the Romans cowered behind their fortifications, fearing the dark forests and open moors; the Britons roamed freely, at home in the wild. *"They are hares and foxes trying to rule over dogs and wolves,"* Boudicca scoffed, turning the Romans into prey and the Britons into predators. A ripple of laughter and fierce joy went through the crowd – the hunter's moon was rising, and they would no longer be the hunted. Her metaphor was more than insult; it was sacred symbolism. In Celtic lore, every creature carries meaning. By calling the Romans lowly animals and the Britons noble wolves, Boudicca cast the coming war as part of the natural order: the weaker would be devoured by the stronger in accordance with nature's law.

As torches guttered and the moon peaked, Boudicca concluded her speech with a dramatic omen. She reached into the folds of her cloak and drew forth a living hare. With a prayer to the gods, she released the frightened creature into the clearing. Dozens of eyes followed the hare as it bolted into the underbrush. A sudden cheer erupted: it ran to the right –

the auspicious side by Druidic tradition. The Britons believed the direction of a creature's flight foretold the battle's outcome, just as Romans took omens from the flight of birds. The rightward dash of the hare meant divine favour. Exultant shouts echoed in the night. In that charged moment, Boudicca lifted her arms to the sky, face radiant in the moonlight, and called upon her goddess:

"I thank you, Andraste, and call upon you as woman speaking to woman... I beg you for victory and preservation of liberty!"

All around, warriors clashed their swords on shields in wild agreement. "Andraste! Andraste!" they cried, invoking the goddess of victory. Here was a feminine lineage laid bare: a mortal queen appealing to a mother goddess as one strong woman to another, on behalf of her people. Boudicca's prayer was intensely personal – *woman to woman* – yet it carried the weight of an entire nation's yearning for freedom. She presented herself not as a distant monarch but as a daughter of the goddess, equal in womanhood, pleading for her children's survival. This scene crystallized an essential aspect of Brittonic tradition: the sacred feminine stood at the heart of the struggle. Men and women alike saw their fight not just as a military revolt, but as a holy war led by a warrior queen in concert with a goddess.

As the cheers subsided, Boudicca's eyes swept over her assembly. In that moonlit council, prophecy hung in the air. Many later claimed that a glow surrounded the queen as she spoke, an aura of Andraste's presence. Others swore they heard an owl (the night-omen of wisdom) cry out at the very moment the hare vanished into the brush, as if the goddess answered Boudicca's call. Whether these claims were memory or myth, it is certain that Boudicca's speech ignited a spiritual fervour. The chiefs departed that night carrying torches back to their villages – literal and figurative flames of rebellion. Across the land, mothers told children of the queen's dream and the omen of the hare. Elders murmured that the old prophecy was being fulfilled: that a time of reckoning had come when a woman would lead the tribes to cast off the foreign yoke. Under the waxing moon, warriors sharpened swords and sang war-songs to Andraste, believing the goddess of the Britons marched with them.

The Prophetic and Tribal Meaning of Her Words:

Boudicca's speech was more than an act of leadership; it was a mystical manifesto for her people. Each element of her address resonated deeply with tribal identity, feminine lineage, and prophecy. When she spoke of freedom vs. slavery, she tapped into the collective soul of the tribes – the memory of living free on their own terms. In an oral culture like the Celts', where bards endlessly retold the deeds of ancestors, the ideal of freedom was almost mythic. By reminding them how the Romans had despoiled their land and bodies, Boudicca framed their rebellion as a mission to restore cosmic balance. To Celtic thinking, injustice upset the harmony between tribe, earth, and gods. Thus, throwing off Roman oppression was not just revenge – it was setting the world right again, an essentially spiritual act.

Her emphasis on leaving real freedom to their children gave her words a prophetic weight. She made the warriors imagine generations yet unborn casting judgment on them. Would those future Britons live free under the open sky or as slaves under the Roman lash? In invoking the children's freedom, Boudicca was claiming the mantle of a seeress, one who speaks for destiny. Many warriors likely saw in her not only a queen, but a prophet of the tribes' future. This sense of *fate unfolding* was bolstered by the omens she cited. The accounts say that even before the revolt, Heaven gave signs of the catastrophe to come: strange voices in the Roman forum, phantom shouts in the amphitheater, and the Thames appearing to run with blood. Such portents, recorded even by Roman historians, convinced the Britons that the gods had taken a stand. Boudicca became the living instrument of that divine will, the one who would make the prophecy tangible.

Tribal identity: One of Boudicca's most powerful symbolic acts was to collapse the walls between tribes. Normally, Britons were fiercely loyal to their own clan or kingdom. Yet Boudicca addressed all Britons as one – *"you inhabit a single island and are called by one common name"*. In doing so, she evoked the ancient concept of Albion – the idea that the island itself has a singular spirit and that all its children are bound together. This was a radical notion, and profoundly spiritual. To the Celts, the land was alive; hills and rivers had guardian deities, and the very soil carried the memory of their ancestors. By appealing to a pan-Britannic identity, Boudicca in effect summoned the spirit of the island to her cause. Each warrior, whether from the Iceni, Trinovantes, or others, could feel that the soul of Britannia was on their side, and that in uniting, they became part of something larger and eternal – the tribe of tribes. It turned the war into a sacred duty to their motherland.

Feminine lineage: Boudicca's role as a woman leader was not an anomaly but deeply rooted in Briton tradition. It was said that Britons did not distinguish gender in matters of leadership, and that queens or female druids could hold sway when the time called for it. Indeed, the Roman historian Tacitus notes that Britons made no distinction of sex in their royal succession and that *"it was not unusual for them to fight under the leadership of women."* Boudicca's own name, derived from the Brythonic word *boudi* (victory), literally means "Victorious Woman" – perhaps a prophetic naming by her parents, as if in anticipation of her destiny. In her speech, Boudicca consciously draws on this feminine power. When she says *"I am a woman avenging my lost freedom, my scourged body, and the outraged chastity of my daughters,"* she makes her womanhood the very source of her wrath and authority. Rather than weakening her, her identity as mother and violated matron gives her a terrible strength that the tribes revered. In their spiritual worldview, a mother defending her young or a woman defending her honor was a force of nature – like a she-wolf whose cubs are threatened.

Furthermore, Boudicca invoked a mythic sisterhood by referencing legendary queens. In Cassius Dio's account, she boldly contrasts herself with queens of older empires: *"I rule over no soft Egyptians as did Nitocris, nor traders as did Semiramis... much less over Romans as Messalina or Agrippina did"*. By naming Nitocris (a semi-legendary queen of ancient Egypt) and Semiramis (the warrior-queen of Assyria), as well as the notorious Roman empresses, Boudicca places herself in a long line of powerful women rulers known to history. However, she invokes them only to reject their model: unlike those women who ruled decadent civilisations or tyrannical courts, Boudicca rules wild free Britons – people who *"know not how to till the soil or trade, but are versed in the art of war"*, where even the women fight alongside the men. This juxtaposition is striking. It's as if Boudicca is saying: *I come from a purer lineage of warrior women, one that answers not to imperial luxury but to the call of the earth and the blade.* She declares that among her people, women possess the same valor as men, and thus she stands not above her tribe but with them, as a warrior in spirit as much as a queen. This rhetoric would have deeply stirred a society accustomed to honoring strong women – from the semi-divine queens of myth to the wise old chief's widow who might arbitrate disputes. It affirmed that the feminine and the martial were not opposed, but united in their cause.

In that council beneath the moon, Boudicca embodied the triple role of womanhood revered in Celtic tradition: Maiden, Mother, and Crone – she was a maiden in her purity of purpose, a mother in her fierce protection of her daughters (and by extension her people), and a wise elder (crone) in channeling ancestral wisdom and prophecy. The presence of her daughters in the chariot during her speeches was itself symbolic. They were not hidden away but displayed, their very existence a reminder of Rome's atrocity and the lineage of warrior women that would continue after Boudicca. As she spoke of liberty, those two young women stood as living prophecies of the future – if the Britons failed, those girls would either die or live as slaves; if the Britons triumphed, they would inherit a free land. Thus the feminine lineage – from goddess, to queen, to daughters – was invoked as the thread connecting past, present, and future in the tapestry of the rebellion.

Prophecy and mysticism: Celtic culture prized its seers and prophets, and Boudicca in her speech acted as one. The releasing of the hare was more than a clever morale trick; it was a sacred act of divination. In that moment, Boudicca became the oracle of Andraste, interpreting the goddess's will through the hare's path. To the warriors, the favourable omen meant their victory was preordained by the gods. This belief would have made them nearly fearless in battle – they saw themselves as fulfilling a prophecy. Moreover, by thanking Andraste publicly for her guidance, Boudicca essentially declared that the goddess had spoken through her. It gave her an aura of holy authority. Any who doubted the rebellion need only look at the outcome of the omen to be convinced that the campaign had divine sanction.

There was likely another layer of prophecy circulating: some have speculated that druidic prophecies or local soothsayers had foretold a time of cleansing war when the Britons would rise against invaders. Roman writers noted that as Boudicca's revolt broke out, the statue of Victory in the Roman colony fell down inexplicably and women in trance-like frenzy chanted about ruin to come. What the Romans interpreted as ill omens, the Britons could interpret as confirmation of Boudicca's destined role. Indeed, Boudicca's very name meaning "Victorious" seemed a prophecy in itself. Many must have felt it was no coincidence that a woman literally named Victory was chosen to lead them against Rome's legions. In an esoteric sense, Boudicca *was* the prophecy walking on two legs – the embodiment of Britain's yearning for freedom and the manifestation of the goddess's wrath.

Thus, every word of Boudicca's rallying speech carried a double weight: one in the temporal realm of strategy and justice, and one in the spiritual realm of destiny and symbolism. She spoke as a Briton, but also as a vessel of the Great Mother's voice. The council of chiefs became not just a war meeting but a kind of ceremonial gathering, in which oaths were sworn under the moon and a covenant was made between the people and their gods. In Boudicca's stirring words, the tribal past met the prophetic future – and the Britons stepped across that threshold, united, inspired, and ready to write legend with their swords.

Andraste: Goddess of Victory and the Moon

When Boudicca cried out "I thank you, Andraste... I beg you for victory and liberty," she was invoking a deity fervently worshipped among the Iceni: Andraste, the war-goddess of Britain. To understand the spiritual fire behind Boudicca's revolt, one must know Andraste, for the queen and the goddess were inextricably linked in the minds of the people. Andraste (also referred to as Andrasta in some sources) was known as the goddess of victory to the Iceni and their allies. Roman observers even noted that Andraste was *"their name for Victory"*, equating her with the Roman goddess Victoria. This suggests that the Britons personified victory itself as a divine female presence – a spirit that could be propitiated and entreated to favor them in war.

The name "Andraste" carries the meaning of invincibility – it has been translated as "indestructible" or "unconquerable". In that name lies her essence: Andraste was the Unconquerable One, embodying the resilience and fighting spirit of the tribes. Some scholars believe she may have been related to a broader Celtic goddess known in Gaul as Andarta, possibly meaning "Great/Bear Goddess" or similarly "powerful". In either case, the sense is of a mighty protectress who cannot be vanquished. It is tantalising to think that Boudicca – whose own name means "Victorious Woman" – was perhaps seen by her people as an earthly reflection of the goddess Andraste. Indeed, when the rebellion erupted, Dio records that Boudica called upon Andraste to aid her army. To her warriors, the queen was fighting *with* the goddess, almost as if Andraste rode into battle in Boudicca's chariot.

Origins and Worship: Andraste's origins are shrouded in the mists of pre-Roman Britain. Unlike gods of the classical pantheon, she was not written about until the Romans took notice during Boudicca's war. We know of her mainly through the likes of Cassius Dio, who noted her invocation and the ferocity of her cult. As a war goddess, Andraste was likely honored in sacred groves and forest sanctuaries rather than in built temples. The Britons held woodlands to be the holiest of places – the chief shrines of their gods. In fact, after one of Boudicca's victories, the rebels held celebratory rites *"not only in all their other sacred places, but particularly in the grove of Andate"* (Andate being another name for Andraste/Victory). This grove of Andraste was evidently a central place of worship, where the Britons gave thanks to the goddess for their triumphs. Cassius Dio chillingly describes how the Britons sacrificed to Andraste in that grove: Roman captives, especially high-born women, were offered up in gruesome ways – hung naked, their severed breasts offered to the goddess, and their bodies impaled – all "to the accompaniment of sacrifices, banquets, and wanton behaviour". As horrific as this is to our eyes, to the Britons it was the ultimate act of devotional fury: a blood offering to the goddess who had granted them victory. It underscores the primeval intensity of Andraste's worship. She was no gentle deity of the hearth; she was the Warrior Maiden who thirsted for the blood of the tribe's enemies.

Symbols associated with Andraste hint at her character and perhaps her domain over the moon and night. One creature stands out: the hare. Later traditions (and many neopagan sources today) hold that the hare was sacred to Andraste. This belief likely stems directly from Boudicca's ritual – the hare released before battle. The hare in Celtic symbolism can represent agility, intuition, and the moon (hares are often associated with lunar deities in various cultures, as their nocturnal activity and cycles of fertility mirror the moon's cycles). When Boudicca said, *"Let us show [the Romans] that they are hares and foxes trying to rule over dogs and wolves,"* she was possibly belittling them, yet interestingly she chose the hare – the creature linked to her goddess – as an image, perhaps implying the Romans were frightened prey scattering before the Britons' wrath. In her prayer, by contrast, the hare becomes a divine messenger. When it ran the "auspicious" way, the Britons believed Andraste was speaking through the animal. We see here a duality: the hare is both hunted and holy, much like the moon which can be a faint, hunted thing in the sky or a bright holy lamp guiding hunters by night.

It is very likely that Andraste was worshipped under the full moon. As a goddess of war and victory, her rituals might precede battle, often launched at first light or under cover of darkness. Imagine the Iceni warriors gathering on the eve of battle: the druids (or priestesses) leading them in a nocturnal rite. Torches would blaze in a circle, drums would beat, and in the center an altar stone might be draped with fresh oak boughs (oak being sacred). A white-clad priestess could invoke Andraste, calling her to fill the warriors with her "unconquerable" essence. Offerings would be made – perhaps a libation of mead poured to the earth, or the ritual slaughter of a rooster or hare – asking the goddess to accept these gifts and grant triumph. The warriors may have danced or chanted her name, working themselves into a trance of courage. Given the evidence, human sacrifice was reserved for after victory (a grim thanksgiving), but prayer and maybe symbolic sacrifices would precede the fight.

Andraste's imagery in the minds of her worshippers may have been fearsome and majestic. Perhaps they envisioned her as a tall, red-haired woman (not unlike Boudicca herself) riding a chariot through the sky, much as the goddess Victoria or Athena Nike was depicted by Romans and Greeks. In fact, it's intriguing that goddesses of victory in Indo-European cultures – Nike, Victoria, the Morrígan to some extent – are often shown or described as riding or flying swiftly, carrying a spear or sword. Andraste might have been seen as racing alongside the Briton armies, her presence detected in the rush of wind that preceded a charge or the crimson sunset that hinted at next morning's battle.

Some accounts hint that Andraste could have also had a lunar or nocturnal aspect. The context of Boudicca's invocation – at night, after the hare's augury – and the fact that many Celtic rituals were timed by the moon, suggest Andraste was comfortable in the moonlight. Diana, the Roman moon goddess, was also a patron of wild hunts and by extension could be linked to warfare in the wild woods. It is possible that Andraste was seen as a moon goddess of battle, one who watched over warriors by night. If the Britons held night marches or ambushes (as native guerrilla fighters often did), they may have prayed to Andraste for the moon's light or darkness as suited their needs. The crescent moon could have been one of her symbols, resembling a silver bow ready to shoot arrows of inspiration into the hearts of the brave.

Diana: Echoes of the Huntress

One of the most fascinating questions about Andraste is how she might connect to more widely known deities – in particular, the Roman Diana (Greek Artemis). During the mythic age of Brutus, as later medieval legends tell, the Trojan hero Brutus (said to be the founder of Britain) sought guidance from none other than the goddess Diana upon reaching the shores of Albion. In those tales, Brutus performs a midnight ritual at the Temple of Diana, and the goddess of the moon and the hunt delivers to him a prophecy of a great kingdom he will found in the western isles. This is a striking story: why would a Trojan invoke Diana specifically for a prophecy about Britain? Some scholars suspect this reflects a conflation or syncretism – that the indigenous Britons' chief goddess was equated with Diana in the retelling. In other words, the storytellers of medieval Britain may have used the name "Diana" for a native Great Goddess of the land, perhaps Andraste or a deity much like her.

Consider the attributes of Diana: she is a huntress, often depicted with a bow, accompanied by wild animals (stags, hounds) and sometimes by a hare or hunting dogs. She is a virgin goddess, fiercely independent, who defends her purity and her companions. She is also a moon goddess, governing the nocturnal realm and the cycles of nature. Now compare Andraste: a virgin war goddess, if we take Boudicca's invocation "woman to woman" to imply that Andraste, like Diana, stands apart from any male consort. Andraste is associated with the wild hunt of war, with warriors as her hounds. She revels in the forests and groves, the natural temples of Britain. And the hare – one of Diana's creatures in Roman art and myth – appears centrally in Andraste's single greatest story. The parallels suggest that when Romans encountered Andraste, they might have seen in her an aspect of their own Artemis/Diana: a peerless maiden of battle and woodlands. Indeed, one classical source explicitly notes that the Britons worshipped "a goddess of victory" and implies she was identified with Roman Victory or Diana, though the lines blur between these classical equivalences.

During Brutus's mythical era (long before Rome's conquest), if we imagine the Celtic tribes in their primal worship, a figure like Andraste would have loomed large. It is easy to picture early Britons telling stories of a moonlit goddess who guarded the island. Perhaps they believed this goddess guided Brutus to their shore, sanctioning the first settlement of the Trojan Britons. If so, by the Roman period, that guardian deity had become firmly entwined with Andraste, the guardian of victory and freedom. Roman interpreters, seeing Britons pray to a powerful female deity, might have written it down as Diana out of familiarity. Even in Boudicca's time, some Britons might themselves have linked Andraste to the concept of the Moon Mother. The moon was crucial to their calendars and rituals (as we will see), so a war goddess who also presided over nights and nature would align well with their cosmology.

There is also an interesting note: the cult of Diana in Roman Britain eventually took hold, especially in cities and Romanised areas, but in the countryside the old Celtic goddesses persisted. At Bath, for instance, the goddess Sul was identified with Minerva by the Romans. One could speculate that in some locales, Andraste was identified with Diana, especially among those who wanted to frame Boudicca's rebellion in terms of Roman mythology. Diana, after all, had famously punished men who wronged her (like Actaeon). To Britons, Andraste was that avenging maiden, punishing the Romans for their arrogance.

In terms of symbolism, by conflating Andraste with Diana one enriches the image of Andraste: we then see her not only as a blood-soaked victory goddess but also as a protectress of the woodlands, the wild creatures, and the cycles of the moon. She becomes a holistic Great Goddess of the Britons – one who can be maidenly and radiant (as the moon) and also terrifying and bloodletting (as the spirit of war). It is possible that during Boudicca's holy war, the Britons believed the moon's phases reflected Andraste's favor. A full moon might be the goddess's lamp guiding them to victory; a lunar eclipse might signify her anger or sorrow. One romantic legend (unverified but often repeated in neopagan circles) claims that Boudicca prayed to Andraste under a full moon before the final battle, vowing that win or lose, she would remain free – which aligns with Tacitus's note that Boudicca said she would not survive enslavement: *"This is a woman's resolve; as for men, they may live and be slaves if they wish."* In that vein, Andraste/Diana becomes the guarantor of a freely chosen death over forced subjugation, a theme very much in keeping with both goddesses' fierce independence.

Thus, Andraste and Diana can be seen as mirror images across cultural lines. In the mythic telling, Diana's prophecy to Brutus set the stage for Britain's founding; in the historic moment, Andraste's prophecy (through Boudicca's vision and the hare's path) nearly altered Britain's fate by casting out Rome. Both are moon-huntress figures overseeing turning points in British story. And in both cases, we see the idea of divine female guidance – something deeply valued in Indo-European traditions where the moon or dawn goddess often guides heroes. In a sense, Andraste was the Britannic Artemis, leading her people through the dark night of oppression toward the hope of a new dawn.

Sisters in Fury: Warrior Goddesses Across Cultures

Andraste did not stand alone in the ancient world. She was one fierce star in a whole constellation of Indo-European warrior goddesses. By comparing her to some of these divine sisters, we gain a richer understanding of the archetype she represents – the Warrior Woman who defends her people and decides battles. Across Celtic lands and beyond, cultures revered such figures, blending the lines between goddess, spirit, and mythic heroine.

- **The Morrígan (Ireland):** Perhaps the closest parallel to Andraste is the Irish Morrígan, a complex goddess (often appearing as a trio of sisters) who presides over war and fate. The Morrígan is known as the "Phantom Queen" and is often interpreted as a war goddess. She famously appears on battlefields as a raven or crow, flying overhead to inspire fear or courage in warriors, and she has the power of prophecy – foretelling who will live or die. Like Andraste, the Morrígan exults in the frenzy of battle; one medieval Irish tale describes her as deriving pleasure from the carnage of war. She also has a protective aspect: scholars note she is a guardian of the land and its people, ensuring their prosperity and sovereignty by defending them in war. During the legendary Cattle Raid of Cooley, the Morrígan confronted the hero Cú Chulainn multiple times, shifting shapes from a maiden to an eel to a wolf to a crone, testing and aiding and dooming warriors in turn. This shape-shifting, war-fury goddess who washes the armour of those about to die is a spiritual cousin to Andraste. Both represent the belief that the divine feminine actively weaves the fate of battle, and both are invoked by warriors seeking victory. We might imagine that on the spiritual plane, Morrígan and Andraste were two faces of a pan-Celtic war goddess, each attending to her own land's battles – one in Hibernia (Ireland) and one in Britannia – perhaps watching each other's works with interest as their peoples fought for survival.

- **Cathubodua (Gaul):** In the Celtic regions of Gaul (modern France), the Romans recorded the worship of Cathubodua, a name which literally translates to

"Battle Crow." This deity is likely the Gaulish equivalent of the Morrígan/Badb. The crow, of course, is a bird of the battlefield, scavenging among the dead, and also a harbinger of doom. If Cathubodua was invoked in Gaul, she certainly shares DNA with Andraste's cult – emphasising the ravenous, blood-thirsty aspect of war. We have less detail about her rituals, but it's plausible that, like the Britons, the continental Celts honored their war goddess with trophies of their enemies. A warrior setting out to fight might pray to Cathubodua or Andraste for the strength of the crow – to be the devourer, not the devoured. The consistency of a crow goddess across Celtic Europe suggests that the idea of a female battle-spirit was deeply ingrained, perhaps stemming from an older Indo-European myth of a warrior bird-goddess.

- **Brigantia (Britain):** Closer to home, the Brigantes tribe of northern Britain worshipped a goddess named Brigantia. While primarily a sovereignty and prosperity goddess, Brigantia was identified by the Romans with Minerva, and depictions show her with warlike attributes (helmet, spear, shield) – effectively as a warrior-protectress of her people. An inscription even calls upon "Brigantia the Victory-bringer." She thus shares Andraste's victorious aspect. Brigantia's name is cognate with Brigid (the exalted one) and hints at a lofty status; she likely governed statecraft and defense for the Brigantes. We see in Brigantia another example of how Celtic peoples merged the idea of territorial goddess and war goddess – she who is the land (sovereignty) also defends the land (war). Andraste might well have been a similar fusion for the Iceni: the personal deity of the Iceni tribe's territory, invoked in times of war to guard her children.

- **Athena (Greece) & Bellona (Rome):** The concept of a warrior goddess was not unique to Celts. In the Greek pantheon, Athena embodies strategic warfare and the protection of the city. Though different in temperament (Athena is a cool-headed strategist, whereas Andraste is a fiery battle-fury), Athena's role as a female martial deity who aids her favoured heroes in battle echoes the kind of divine aid Boudicca sought from Andraste. Both goddesses are depicted as virginal (never mastered by any male god) and often as saviours in crises. Meanwhile, the Romans had Bellona, literally "War" personified as a goddess, who was often depicted armed and armoured. Roman generals would invoke Bellona for success in war, and a temple to Bellona in Rome saw ceremonies where a spear was hurled to symbolically begin war. Bellona could be seen as a Roman analog to Andraste – indeed, when Dio lists goddesses related to Victoria, he includes Bellona and Magna Mater (Cybele), both ferocious female powers. The difference is that Bellona was more a representation of Mars's power, whereas Andraste was uniquely the Britons' own. Still, these parallels show that Indo-European cultures frequently envisioned war in feminine form – perhaps recognising that war is not just brute strength (a male attribute often), but also contains elements of fate, frenzy, protection, and inspiration, which they ascribed to female divinities.

- **Durga/Kali (Hindu tradition):** Even far to the east in the Indo-European family, in ancient Vedic and Hindu belief, we find goddesses like Durga and Kali who ride out to battle demons and preserve cosmic order. Durga is depicted with weapons in many arms, slaying the buffalo-demon, much as a warrior might slay a wild foe; Kali, with her garland of skulls and bloodied tongue, revels in the destruction of evil forces – terrifying but ultimately protective. These goddesses, like Andraste, require blood offerings in some stories and embody the idea that the divine feminine can be ferocious. They also illustrate the theme of prophecy and fate – Kali's dance can bring about the end of ages if not checked. While there was no contact between Celtic Druids and Hindu priests, it is remarkable that from the Ganges to the Thames, cultures understood the two-sided nature of womanhood in myth: nurturing on one hand, and utterly devastating when that nurture is threatened. Boudicca, invoking Andraste, tapped into this primal archetype of the avenging mother/protectress that resonates across time and   place.

- **Valkyries and Freyja (Norse):** In the Norse-Germanic sphere, war had its goddesses too. The Valkyries were choosers of the slain, eerie maidens who flew over battles and selected which warriors would die and be taken to Valhalla. They share the bird-woman imagery with the Celtic Morrígan (often described as swan maidens or equipped with falcon cloaks) and the fateful influence on battle outcome. And Norse mythology's Freyja, though primarily a fertility and love goddess, also claims half of the heroic dead to her own hall and is said to ride into battle when needed; like Andraste, she could be seen as a goddess who empowers warriors and receives their souls. These parallels show a common thread: many Indo-European societies personified the chaos and fate of war in female form, perhaps as a counterbalance to the male warrior ideal. The female war deity or spirit often brings the crucial element of luck or destiny – something no sword can fight against.

In summary, Andraste can be viewed alongside Badb/Morrígan, Athena, Bellona, Durga, Freyja and others as part of an ancient sisterhood of war. Each culture's version had unique flavour – the Morrígan was also tied to land fertility, Athena to wisdom, Durga to righteousness – yet all share a basic role: galvanising the people in times of war and guiding the outcome in accordance with a higher law. For the Britons, Andraste was *their* fierce goddess, born of their land's spirit. In Boudicca's uprising, they likely felt they were witnessing a scene that had played out in their myths for centuries: the goddess of the land rises through chosen leaders to defend her children, fulfilling the prophecies of old. The archetype of the warrior goddess gave the Britons a framework to interpret their struggle – Boudicca was to them as a hero under Andraste's patronage, much like heroes of Greece under Athena's or Irish heroes under the Morrígan's shadow. This not only validated the rebellion spiritually but also steeled the warriors with legendary courage. After all, if Andraste and her divine sisters were with them, how could mere Roman mortals withstand them?

Moonlit Rites and the Priestesses of Albion

Beyond the battles and the speeches, an essential aspect of ancient British tradition – especially highlighted in Boudicca's story – is the role of feminine-led rituals, moon rites, and ceremonial practices in the spiritual life of the tribes. The Celts of Britain were a deeply spiritual people who wove their religious observances into the fabric of daily life and warfare alike. Women, in particular, often stood at the forefront of these rituals as seeresses, priestesses, and keepers of the lunar calendar. Let us step away from the clamour of battle for a moment and enter the sacred groves and stone circles where, under the argent light of the moon, Britons sought the favour of the gods.

Druidesses and Seeresses: Classical authors usually speak of the Druids – the learned priestly class of the Celts – in male terms, but evidence abounds that women served as seers and even druids among the northern tribes. In neighbouring Gaul, the writer Pomponius Mela described an island (the Isle of Sena, off the coast of Brittany) inhabited by nine virgin priestesses who could foretell the future, heal the sick, and control the weather with their rituals. It's very likely that Britain too had its oracle-women. Indeed, at the very time Boudicca was mustering in the east, a dramatic scene was unfolding in the west: the Roman governor Suetonius led an assault on the island of Mona (Anglesey), the sacred stronghold of the Druids. Tacitus recounts that as Roman troops approached the shore, they were faced not only by armed warriors but by druidesses – women with streaming hair, clad in black like Furies, brandishing torches and screaming curses 【 Tacitus, *Annals* 14.30 】 . The sight, he notes, was so startling that the Roman soldiers froze in fear, mouths agape at these wild prophetesses calling down doom. This account is a rare and precious peek at feminine-led ritual in action: these women were performing a battle rite, invoking (through their frightening appearance and chants) the gods' wrath on the invaders. They acted as living conduits of divine terror, much as Boudicca acted as a conduit of divine inspiration. Eventually the Romans conquered Anglesey, massacring the Druids and their women, and destroying the sacred groves. But the memory of those fearsome priestesses would have lived on among Britons, fuelling a desire for revenge – and perhaps inspiring Boudicca's own daughters and female followers to take up torches and **sacred chants in her war.

Throughout Britain, women played vital roles in ritual life. They kept the household altars, maintaining the small fires and offerings to the family deities and ancestral spirits. They were also often the healers and herb-wives, knowing the properties of plants by heart, dispensing remedies alongside prayers to goddesses like Brigid or Sul. Many a chieftain's wife or daughter was also taught the arts of augury (interpreting signs) and poetry, for poetry itself was a sacred art of the bards, and not solely male – we have names of a few Celtic poetesses. On the eve of battle, it may have been women who prepared the war band's feasting and ritual purification – painting the warriors with blue woad dye in swirling patterns (a quasi-ritual body art), and singing the keening songs that arouse battle-fury or lament those who are about to die.

Moon Rites and the Lunar Calendar: The moon was the clock and compass of the ancient Celts. They divided their year by lunar months, and many of their festivals were tied to lunar events. The Coligny Calendar, a bronze Celtic calendar found in Gaul, shows a complex lunisolar system – evidence that Druids kept close track of the moon's cycles to schedule ceremonies. In Britain, it was likely similar: the word "month" itself comes from "moon-th". Key tribal gatherings and feasts often aligned with certain moon phases. For instance, Samhain, the new year feast (around November), and Beltane (May) might have been observed on the full moon nearest the midpoint between equinox and solstice. The moon was believed to affect crops, fertility, and magic, so timing rituals to the moon was thought to amplify their potency.

One famous ritual described by Pliny the Elder involves Druids harvesting mistletoe – a sacred plant – which had to be done with meticulous timing: *"on the sixth day of the moon, when the moon has grown enough to have considerable strength"*. Clad in white, the Druids would climb an oak, cut the mistletoe with a golden sickle, and let it fall into a white cloth – careful that it not touch the ground – then sacrifice two white bulls in honour of the ceremony. While Pliny's account centres on male Druids, it underscores how the moon's phase was considered crucial for sanctioning sacred work. The "sixth day of the moon" suggests that certain days after the new moon were deemed lucky or imbued with divine force. It's easy to imagine that priestesses too observed such disciplines: perhaps a band of women gathering herbs only under waxing moonlight, or initiating girls into womanhood when the moon was full, signifying the fullness of female power.

Rituals of Warrior Queens and Prophetesses: A warrior queen like Boudicca would have participated in ceremonial observances specific to leadership and war. Before commencing her rebellion, she might have sought the counsel of the Druids or seers. Perhaps an elderly bandraoi (female druid) cast runes or ogam sticks before her, reading in their pattern the likelihood of success. There may have been a ritual bath in a river for purification, with women attendants anointing Boudicca and her weapons, invoking the blessings of water goddesses for protection. In some cultures, leaders underwent a form of shamanic ritual to bond with a totem animal; one could speculate that Boudicca's people might have done something similar – for instance, imbibing a potion of herbs to induce visions of Andraste or of a guiding animal spirit (a wolf, hare, or crow). The involvement of women in these preparatory rites would be natural, given their role as keepers of esoteric knowledge and as representatives of the goddess on earth.

During the campaign, certain nights would call for continuing rites. If the army camped on a hill under stars, they might light a bonfire as a makeshift altar. We know that after early victories, Boudicca's followers feasted and performed sacrifices in Andraste's groves. It is likely priestesses led those ceremonies, offering the captives to the goddess. The frenzy and "wanton behaviour" noted by Dio could indicate something like a Bacchic revelry or trance-dance led by women in honour of Andraste's triumph. Possibly the Ululation of women – that high-pitched ritual wail – echoed through the oak glades as fires burned high with the spoils of the enemy. Such sounds, carrying in the night, would both honour the goddess and strike fear into any Roman hearts that heard them from afar.

Not all ceremonies were blood-soaked. Moon rites could also be gentler observances: On calm nights between battles, perhaps the queen's entourage – including other noblewomen, her daughters, and wise women – gathered to pray for guidance. Picture a circle of women on a hilltop, Boudicca in their midst, passing a drinking horn of mead sun wise (east to west) as they sing an enchanting hymn to the moon. They might call on Andraste or on Brigantia to send dreams of strategy and courage. They might burn fragrant herbs – juniper, thyme, Celtic sage – in a bronze cauldron as an offering, letting the smoke rise to the heavens carrying their prayers. In such intimate moments, away from the clamour of warriors, the sisterhood of the tribe reinforced their unity and drew down the moon's blessing to their cause. These feminine-focused ceremonies balanced the masculine side of war with a nurturing, metaphysical reinforcement – they were knitting a safety net of magic and faith beneath the feet of their fighting men.

Ceremonial practices of the lunar calendar: also governed the agricultural and community life for which the warrior queens fought. While Boudicca was in the field, she knew that back home the elders and women would be celebrating or soon to celebrate Lughnasadh (the summer harvest festival, typically in August) or Imbolc (spring's first stirrings, in February). Even war might pause or be influenced by such times. It's possible Boudicca chose to launch the rebellion after the spring planting was done and before harvest – a window when warriors could leave the fields.

Indeed, her revolt occurred in AD 60/61, which likely saw its height in late spring and summer. If the Britons marked Beltane (May 1), a fire festival of purification and new beginnings, one wonders if as Beltane fires burned that year, they symbolised not just the coming summer but also the burning of Roman Londinium and Camulodunum that was to come. That year, the Beltane fires may have been literal conflagrations of Roman towns – ritual and reality merging.

In these festivals, women carried torches and kindled sacred flames. We have the image of *Beltane maidens* leaping over bonfires for luck, and *Samhain wise-women* guiding the community in ancestral rites. Warrior queens like Boudicca did not divorce themselves from these traditions – they led them. A queen would light the bonfire on Beltane as surely as she'd light the beacon of war. The seeress at Samhain (the Celtic New Year, when the veil between worlds thins) might pronounce oracles about the tribe's future; if Samhain of AD 60 approached, perhaps a prophecy was spoken that the tyranny over the land would soon end.

Humanised Tone – Life in War and Ritual: It's important to remember that these were not just grand rituals, but part of the fabric of daily human life. The same Boudicca who roared like a lioness in battle was also a mother who likely wept in private for the violation of her daughters – and who sought comfort in prayer under the gentle moon. The tribal people, though caught up in a brutal war, still looked to the moon's reassuring cycles to remind them that life goes on and that their world was more than bloodshed. Many a warrior in Boudicca's camp must have taken heart seeing the Moon's rising each night, believing it a sign that Andraste watches over them unblinking. Wounded men were tended by women under that moonlight, their wounds washed with herbal brews as soft songs were sung to ease pain. Children in the migrating war-camp (for surely families trailed or hid while the fighting men marched) would have been shushed to sleep with lullabies that mingled hope and fear – maybe a tune about the moon goddess traveling through the sky, never faltering, just as the Britons must never falter.

Indeed, the moon could be viewed as a symbol of feminine endurance: Though it waxes and wanes, it always returns. Likewise the Britons, even if battered, would rise again. In a poetic sense, "the Moon's Rising" in our chapter title signifies the ascent of the feminine, the resurgence of native tradition and intuition, after a period of darkness. Boudicca's revolt was brief, but it was a bright full moon in the long night of Roman occupation – a moment when the old tribal soul shone in fullest glory.

CONCLUSION

LEGACY OF THE LUNAR QUEEN

Boudicca's stand against Rome was a convergence of history and myth, a moment when a leader's temporal struggle became indistinguishable from a spiritual crusade. In the chapter of Britain's story titled *"Boudicca's Dream and the Moon's Rising,"* we see how the human and the divine, the past and future, the feminine and the martial all met on the field of conflict. Boudicca's dream infused her waking life with purpose, and under the rising moon she forged that purpose into reality with the help of her people and her gods.

In the end, the rebellion did not achieve a lasting military victory – the Roman war machine, though shaken, prevailed in crushing the Britons in a pitched battle. Boudicca, according to Tacitus, took poison rather than be captured; Dio says she fell ill and died, and was given lavish burial rites befitting a heroine. But in a deeper sense, Boudicca and Andraste were victorious. They won immortality. Tribal identity in Britain was never the same – the tribes had united and discovered their collective strength, a memory that would smoulder on, flaring up in later revolts. The feminine lineage of leadership was powerfully affirmed – for generations after, Celtic legend and later British folklore celebrated warrior queens and wise women, from the medieval figure of Queen Cordelia to the Victorian idealisation of Boudicca as a national symbol. And the prophecy of freedom, though delayed, was not forgotten: nearly four centuries later, when Roman rule collapsed, one imagines the Britons whispering that the spirit of Boudicca had arisen once more to reclaim the land for her people.

In the quiet of night, when one stands among the earthwork ruins of an Iceni village or in the shadow of an old oak in an English woodland, one can almost sense them: the queen and the goddess. The moon gleams through the branches, and perhaps, if you close your eyes, you might hear on the wind a woman's voice – proud, defiant, mournful and hopeful all at once – echoing words of old: *"I call upon you as woman speaking to woman... I pray for victory and liberty."* That prayer transcended its moment. It reverberated through history, empowering not only Boudicca's warriors but countless others who would invoke her name as a symbol of resistance. To this day, Boudicca is remembered not just as a queen who fought Rome, but as a folk heroine, almost a semi-deity, a British Athena or Diana who personifies the right of a people to live free.

Her dream lives on as well – the dream of a land where ancestral traditions and identities survive the onslaught of empire, much as the moon persists even when clouds cover it. The Moon's rising in her story is the emergence of that indomitable spirit. Just as the moon goes through dark phases but returns to full brightness, the Britons under Boudicca went through despair and kindled a bright flame of hope. The cycle continued: darkness fell again after her defeat, but the memory of her light guided future Britons in their own struggles.

In the ancient tribal traditions of Britain, as we have seen, the roles of women, prophecy, and the lunar cycle were central. Boudicca's uprising was in many ways the ultimate expression of those traditions: a war fought like a religious rite, led by a woman imbued with visionary inspiration, unfolding in rhythm with omens and nature's signs. It stands as a testament to how deeply the Britons believed that the Otherworld can intercede in this world, that a goddess can spur a humble people to topple statues of Caesars. For a fleeting time, Andraste answered Boudicca's call and the Britons were *almost* free.

Though nearly two millennia separate us from those events, the poetic nuance of Boudicca's tale still resonates. We see a mother turned general, a people's anguish transmuted into courage, and a culture's twilight transformed into legend. Her story, enriched by symbolic interpretation, teaches that the power of spirit and identity can be as potent as swords, and that in the darkest nights, people find solace and strength in their visions – be it a dream of a goddess or the gentle light of the moon. As long as the moon rises over British hills, one might fancy that Boudicca's dream endures – urging each generation to cherish their liberty, honour their lineage, and listen for the quiet voice of the goddess in the rustling leaves, saying *"Stand proud, children of the land."*

Epilogue: The Path Still Hidden

We stand now at the threshold between the past and future, a living bridge to those who walked this land before us. Like our ancestors, we are memory keepers, storytellers, and ritualist, entrusted with the sacred task of carrying forward the whispers of ancient tribes. Our role is profound yet beautifully simple: to remember, to honour, and to awaken the sleeping spirit of the land.

In our modern lives, filled with screens, schedules, and ceaseless distractions, reconnecting with the primal essence of the tribal spirit might feel challenging. Yet beneath our bustling cities and manicured landscapes, the wild, untamed soul of Albion persists. It waits patiently in the rustle of ancient trees, the quiet ripple of a hidden stream, the distant call of a hawk, and the hushed stillness of the moonlit earth.

Tribal fetishes—objects imbued with symbolic power—once acted as bridges between the seen and unseen worlds for our ancestors. Carved stones, sacred bones, feathered amulets, and polished antlers were cherished not merely as objects, but as vessels of spiritual connection and ancestral wisdom. Each tribe's fetish held unique meanings and purposes: protection, divination, healing, or communion with deities and spirits of the land. These objects were charged through ritual, song, dance, and ceremony, binding physical form to the sacred and intangible.

Today, we too can forge our own fetishes. They might be stones carefully selected from a sacred site, feathers gifted by the winds, wood gently taken from fallen branches, or pendants bearing the carved symbols of our lineage. Charged with intention, held in our rituals, and spoken to with reverence, these modern fetishes become anchors, grounding us in our ancestral roots and guiding us through life's complexities. They remind us that we, like our ancestors, are intertwined with a greater, sacred story.

Storytelling, the heartbeat of tribal culture, was never mere entertainment. It was a sacred practice, preserving wisdom, morals, prophecies, and spiritual teachings. Stories carried history and lineage, honouring heroes, queens, druids, and gods. They shaped identities, strengthened community bonds, and offered guidance through life's transitions and challenges. Today, we must reclaim storytelling as an act of remembrance and reconnection. Share stories around fires, in family circles, or at community gatherings. Let these narratives flow freely, infused with humour, sorrow, triumph, and truth. Each retelling becomes a fresh invocation of ancient spirits, bringing the past vividly into the present.

Our ancestors understood that the land itself is alive, speaking in languages of wind, rain, and earth. Ritual, ceremony, and seasonal celebrations were woven around the cycles of nature—solstices, equinoxes, planting, harvesting, and moon phases. Re-establishing these practices means consciously engaging with nature's rhythms once more. Mark the turning of seasons with bonfires and feasts, observe the moon's phases with quiet meditation and prayer, and plant seeds not only in gardens but also in hearts, setting intentions for growth and healing.

Walk the ancient paths again. Visit sacred sites with humility and openness. Touch stones that were set down thousands of years ago, and feel the timeless pulse within them. Let the land speak directly to your heart, revealing insights no text can provide. Remember that land rights extend beyond legality—your connection to ancestral lands is symbolic and spiritual, a living testament to those who came before and those who will follow.

As we reawaken these traditions, let us remember we do not merely replicate ancient rituals—we breathe new life into them, adapting them to heal, empower, and guide us today. Our ceremonies will reflect both continuity and evolution, honouring ancestors while embracing our contemporary journeys.

And so, reader, I invite you to step forward with courage. Become the storyteller, the ritualist, the guardian of sacred objects and sacred earth. Light your fires, sing your songs, dance beneath moon and stars, and listen for the ancient voices whispering in the wind. The path may yet be hidden, but it reveals itself to those who walk with intention, reverence, and open hearts.

Stand now beneath the sky of Albion, feel the pulse of ancestral memories rising through your bones. You are the living flame. You are the thread in a tapestry begun millennia ago. Carry it proudly, pass it gently, and never let it fade. Together, let us keep the old ways alive, walking the hidden path until it is hidden no more.

APPENDIXES

APPENDIX A

VISUAL MAP OF THE TRIBES

Included within these pages is a detailed visual map outlining the territories of the ancient British tribes, with particular emphasis on the Durotriges, their sacred lands, and adjoining regions of southwestern Britain. This map serves as a visual guide to reconnect with ancestral geography, enhancing understanding of the tribes and their spiritual landscapes.

.PPENDIX B:

TRIBAL NAMES, MEANINGS, AND TOTEMS

- **Durotriges:** Meaning "fort dwellers" or "hill-fort people," symbolised by the hare and crescent moon.

- **Iceni:** Meaning "People of the horse," symbolised by the horse and chariot.

- **Brigantes:** Meaning "High Ones," symbolised by the raven or crow.

- **Trinovantes:** Meaning "The vigorous ones," symbolised by the boar.

- **Catuvellauni:** Meaning "Warriors," symbolised by the wolf.

- **Dobunni:** Meaning "Deep ones," symbolised by the water and salmon.

This concise list helps decode the symbolic language and cultural significance held by each tribe, offering keys for contemporary spiritual practices and identification with ancestral symbolism.

APPENDIX C

RITUAL TEMPLATES AND CHANTS

Invocation of the Four Directions:

East, Hawk of vision clear, Air, whisper your guidance near. South, Adder of fire's dance, Bring change, courage, new chance. West, Hare of water flow, Teach us magic, help us grow. North, Toad of silent earth, Wisdom guide our spiritual birth.

Ancestor Honouring Ritual:

- Prepare a sacred space facing north.

- Place symbolic items representing your ancestors.

- Light a candle, softly invoking ancestral presence.

- Speak personal words of gratitude or traditional blessings.

- Meditate quietly, feeling ancestral support and guidance.

These ritual templates and chants offer practical ways to enact ancient traditions within modern contexts, enabling authentic reconnection with ancestral spirituality.

APPENDIX D

FURTHER READING AND SOURCES

For those inspired to delve deeper into the tribal lore, mythology, and history of Britain, the following texts offer enriching insights:

- **The Celtic Myths: A Guide to the Ancient Gods and Legends** by Miranda Aldhouse-Green.

- **Blood and Mistletoe: The History of the Druids in Britain** by Ronald Hutton.

- **Boudica: Iron Age Warrior Queen** by Richard Hingley and Christina Unwin.

- **Celtic Spirituality: Classics of Western Spirituality** edited by Oliver Davies.

- **The Ancient Paths: Discovering the Lost Map of Celtic Europe** by Graham Robb.

www.ingramcontent.com/pod-product-compliance
Lightning Source LLC
Chambersburg PA
CBHW051144120626
46547CB00012B/932